Surveying the Land

Skills and Exercises in U.S. Historical Geography
Volume 1: To 1877

Robert B. Grant
Framingham State College

D.C. Heath and Company
Lexington, Massachusetts   Toronto

Address editorial correspondence to:

D. C. Heath and Company
125 Spring Street
Lexington, MA 02173

Acquisitions Editor: James Miller
Developmental Editor: Sylvia Mallory
Production Editor: Rosemary Jaffe
Designer: Kenneth Hollman
Production Coordinator: Charles Dutton
Permissions Editor: Margaret Roll

Maps: Boston Graphics, Inc.

Cover Illustration by Raymond Yu, PandaMonium Designs

Published simultaneously in Canada.

Printed in the United States of America.

International Standard Book Number: 0-669-27111-X

10 9 8 7 6 5 4 3 2 1

Foreword

"History takes place in places," said a wise professor who was good at pointing out the obvious—and the often overlooked. Students of history sometimes get so caught up in considering social and political matters that they give insufficient attention to taking a close look at physical place. Yet climate and elevation, soil quality and adequacy of water, coastlines and river systems, and other features of physical context play major roles in historical change and development.

This book is intented to help you sharpen your sense of place and develop an appreciation of the geographical features that so influence historical change. Part I, "Exploring the Physical Environment Through Maps," summarizes major geographic terms and concepts useful to the student of history or to anyone with a curious mind. Part II, "The United States: A Geographic and Climatic Portrait," considers the broad geographic features and characteristics of the United States as a whole, its political boundaries, its rivers and mountains, and its climatic regions. The text of Part II discusses these characteristics and provides a synopsis of major events in the expansion of the United States since the colonial period. The maps in Part II are referred to again and again throughout the book. They offer an overall picture of the political, physiographic, natural vegetation, and rainfall and temperature features of the nation. Answering the questions in Part II will give you a broad overview of these national characteristics. Finally, Part III, "Exercises," comprises thirty-two units focusing on the interaction of history and geography. You are asked to read the text, mark up the maps, and contemplate and answer related questions. The questions in Part III are grouped as Map Exercises and Further Exercises in conjunction with the discussion of each topic. You should be able to deal with the former on the basis of what you have learned from the lectures and reading in your U.S. history course, including this book, and from general knowledge. As their name suggests, the Further Exercises go further. They ask you to consider and investigate matters that may require you to delve beyond your course's content. Your instructor may tell you specifically how to complete the exercises. If he or she chooses not to, you ought to take some pains to work them, especially the Map Exercises, to get the greatest benefit from this book.

Only through using maps will you, as a student of history, develop an adequate concept of place and a good understanding of geographic forces. I hope that you will experience pleasure as well as learning in doing the map exercises in this book.

R. B. G.

Contents

Part I

Introduction: Exploring the Physical Environment Through Maps

History studies change and development over time and how and why change occurs. It considers how people make decisions and take actions and how others react to these initiatives. Because events have a physical locus, "doing" history involves paying close attention to geography, the study of relationships between people and their physical environment. Only a moment's reflection reveals how profoundly the physical environment has influenced history. Suppose that there were a water passage between North and South America. What if Columbus had sailed through it? Suppose there were a major mountain barrier on the eastern coast of North America just as there is on the western coast of South America. Would its presence have altered the development of the English colonies? This Introduction explores the key geographic concepts necessary for an understanding of historical events—and particularly, an understanding of the history of the United States.

Location

To understand events on the planet earth, the history student first must be able to specify the location of those events accurately. The earth's spherical shape makes describing locations difficult. There are no corners or edges to serve as reference points. So geographers use an artificial grid, or network of lines, based on the earth's physical characteristics, to establish location. The earth has an axis—an imaginary line extending through its center. The ends of the earth's axis are the poles, north and south. They are important reference points in the grid. The earth rotates on its axis, making one complete rotation every 24 hours. As it turns, one-half of the planet faces toward the sun and is in daylight, while the other half remains in darkness. The earth also revolves around the sun, taking approximately 365¼ days to make a complete revolution.

The equator is an imaginary line drawn around the globe halfway between the North and South poles, dividing the earth into the Northern and Southern hemispheres. Other imaginary lines circle the earth parallel to the equator and on both sides of it. These are parallels, or lines of latitude. Because of the earth's spherical shape, geographers can measure our planet around, as a circle, with 360 degrees. Each hemisphere therefore measures 180 degrees. The distance between the equator and the North Pole, half of the Northern Hemisphere, measures 90 degrees. The lines of latitude north of the equator mark off the number of degrees of north latitude, from 1 to 90. The system of counting works similarly in the opposite direction. One

1

degree of latitude measures approximately 70 miles, so that at a distance of approximately 140 miles south of the equator is the imaginary line of 2 degrees south latitude, often written 2°S.

To complete the system for determining location, geographers need a second set of imaginary lines to cross the first in a north-south direction and thereby to complete the grid. These are meridians, or lines of longitude. All pass through the two poles and are, therefore, unlike lines of latitude, neither parallel nor equidistant along the length of the line. The lines are farthest apart at the equator, and all intersect at the poles. Agreement at an international conference of astronomers in 1884 established that the meridian that passes through the Royal Observatory in Greenwich, England, would serve as 0 degrees longitude and be designated the prime meridian. Directly opposite on the other side of the globe lies the 180 degree meridian. As the equator divides the earth into Northern and Southern hemispheres, the prime meridian and the 180 degree meridian divide the earth into Eastern and Western hemispheres. Locations east of the prime meridian are designated in degrees of east longitude, with a similar arrangement to the west. Bakersfield, California, for example, is at 119 degrees west longitude, or 119°W.

The intersections of the grid are used to establish location. Because each degree can be subdivided into 60 minutes, and each minute into 60 seconds, a very precise location can be determined. The Statue of Liberty, for example, is at 40 degrees 41 minutes 22 seconds north latitude and 70 degrees 40 minutes 24 seconds west longitude, or 40° 41′ 22″N. and 70° 40′ 24″W.

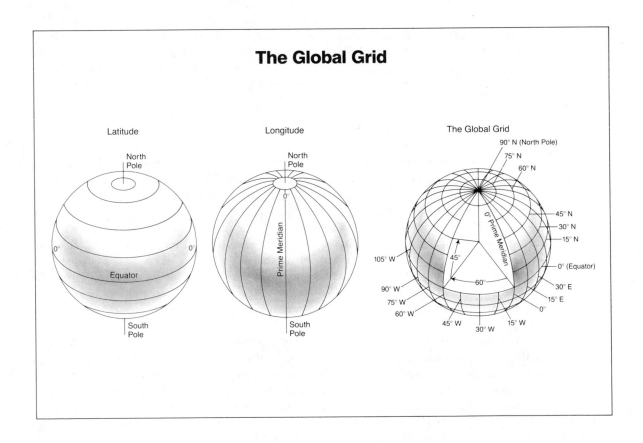

The Global Grid

Time Zones

Time zones are also a matter of importance for the student of history. Because of the earth's rotation, the sun *seems* to circle it every 24 hours. That is, the sun "passes over" or the earth turns through 1/24 of 360 degrees—15 degrees—every hour. When it is noon in one place, it is also noon everywhere else on the same meridian. Fifteen degrees farther west, it is an hour earlier; fifteen degrees to the east, an hour later. For each degree of latitude away from the equator, the size of the degree of longitude diminishes. At New Orleans, Louisiana, for example, one degree equals about 60 miles, but at Ottawa, Ontario, in Canada, it is only about 49 miles.

To ensure being on time, travelers moving east or west would have to adjust their timepieces every few minutes. To avoid this inconvenience and to establish uniformity, standard time zones have been created. Each zone is fifteen degrees wide and represents an area that the sun crosses over in one hour. For the sake of uniformity, all points within the zone are assumed to be at the zone's central meridian. There are 24 time zones around the earth. An obvious problem arises when one gets back to the starting point. To solve it, the 180th meridian has been designated the International Date Line. A traveler going east or west changes dates by a day in either direction. Proceeding east, the traveler has two days of the same date. Moving west, he or she loses one day.

Historians are faced with the problem of time in dating events, especially in earlier centuries. The United States has used standard time zones since the General Time Convention, agreed to by the railroads in 1883 to eliminate problems in printed schedules caused by the unsystematic setting of local times. Congress made the standards official in 1918.

Map Projections

A globe or map provides a visual representation of the earth or a portion of it. A globe may be mounted on a central rod or axis to enable a viewer to spin it and examine its surface. A globe, however, not only is inconveniently bulky, but it cannot simultaneously show two points on opposite sides of the earth. Although this latter problem is overcome through the use of a flat map, a map is merely a two-dimensional representation of a three-dimensional spherical object. And inevitably, all maps have some distortion. Generally speaking, the smaller the area being mapped, the less the distortion.

Cartographers, or mapmakers, draw maps for various purposes and have devised various methods for projecting the earth's curved surface onto a flat map. The choice of projection depends on which features the cartographer wishes to render as free as possible of distortion. One of the oldest of projections, the Mercator, dates back to the sixteenth century. The Mercator stretches the lines of latitude and longitude and thus keeps shapes nearly true, but not size or area. Consequently, land masses near the poles appear larger than they are. Greenland, for example, looks larger than South America in a Mercator projection. The shapes of the two land masses, but not their sizes, are similar to their shapes on a globe. One of the most important qualities of the Mercator projection is that it keeps directions true. Ocean navigators can use it to plot a true course at sea.

There are three basic projections by which to represent the spherical surface of the earth on a flat surface—cylindrical, conical, and planar (azimuthal). In all three, the globe must be placed in relation to both the projection surface and a source of light, and the light "projects" the features of the globe onto the flat map surface. In a cylindrical projection like the Mercator, the cartographer projects onto a cylindrical surface. In the second type of projection, the conical, of which the Lambert conic projection is an example, the cartographer focuses on only a part of the world, usually a country or region in the middle latitudes. If you imagine a cone-shaped hat placed over either pole so that the hat's sides extend down over a part of the globe, you can grasp how the Lambert projection works. That portion of the globe touched by the hat is represented on a flat surface. That is the map. Its top and bottom may be slightly distorted, but the middle portion is fairly true.

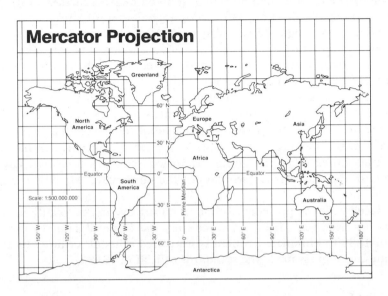

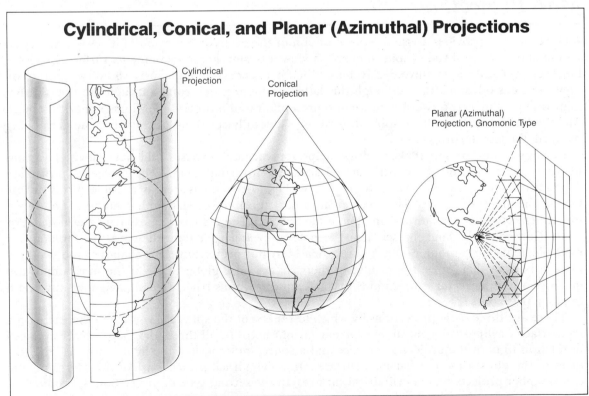

The third basic method of representing the spherical surface of the globe on a flat map is by projecting onto a plane surface tangent to the globe at any point. Planar, or azimuthal, projections differ according to the location of the light source. When the light source is at infinity, all the light rays are parallel. This type of azimuthal projection is called orthographic. In the stereographic projection, the light source is at a point on the globe's surface directly opposite the tangent point. With the gnomonic projection, the light source is at the center of the globe. Azimuthal or fixed-point projections are so called because a fixed point becomes the center of the map. Such maps are circular and are particularly useful for aerial navigation. Directions on an azimuthal map are correct but cannot be shown with a compass symbol on a flat map because north and south follow the radiating meridians rather than straight lines.

The cartographer can modify these three basic geometric projections in construction or by mathematical transformation. The objective may be to reduce overall distortion or to shift distortion from the more important to less important areas of the map, or even to interrupt the projection so that noncritical areas absorb the most distortion.

A different kind of projection, the equal-area projection, shows area and relative size accurately but distorts shapes and direction. In the equal-area Mollweide projection, the central meridian is a straight line half the length to scale of the equator. The mapmaker draws the parallels as straight lines at right angles through the central meridian, spacing them more closely toward the poles. Shape distortion thus increases toward the margins at high latitudes, but relative sizes are similar to those on the globe. The mapmaker can use still other projections. The Homolosine, for example, distorts ocean areas to minimize the distortion of the continents, and the Robinson is a compromise technique. Its objective is to reduce major distortion throughout. There is, consequently, a wider distribution of minor distortion.

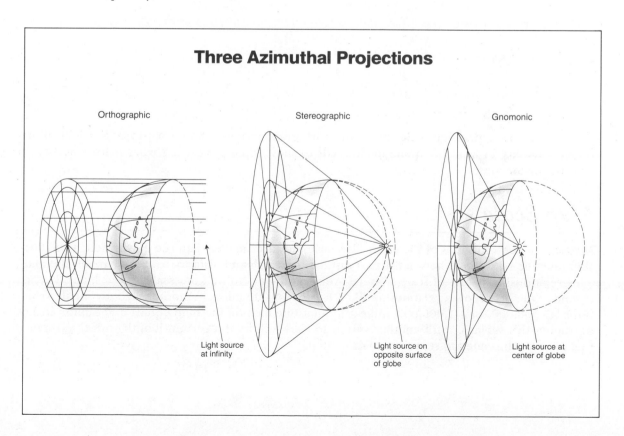

Three Azimuthal Projections

Orthographic

Stereographic

Gnomonic

Light source at infinity

Light source on opposite surface of globe

Light source at center of globe

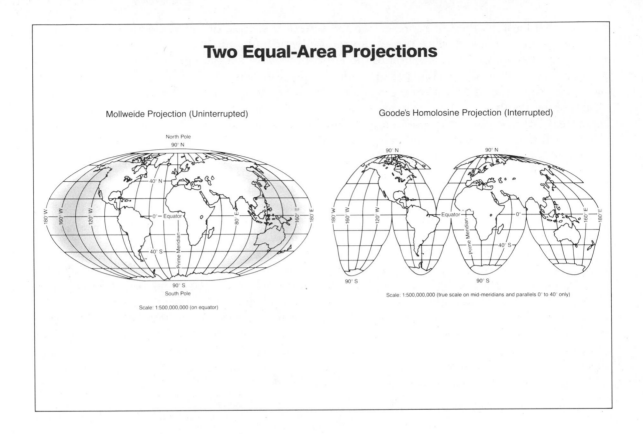

Two Equal-Area Projections

Mollweide Projection (Uninterrupted)

Goode's Homolosine Projection (Interrupted)

Scale: 1:500,000,000 (on equator)

Scale: 1:500,000,000 (true scale on mid-meridians and parallels 0° to 40° only)

To sum up, in drawing a flat map, the cartographer must choose a projection that allows greatest fidelity in what he or she most needs to show while permitting what is least needed to bear the distortion.

Map Scale

Maps are representations of the earth. Because they are smaller than the earth itself, a relationship must be established between actual distance on earth and distance as it appears on the map. This relationship is one of scale. There are several ways to indicate scale in the map's key, or legend. One is to show a relationship like "1 inch = 1,000 miles." Another is to use an abbreviation: 1:1,000,000, or 1/1,000,000, indicating that one inch on the map equals one million inches on the earth's surface. Still another way is to show a line of a certain length with the distance that length is intended to represent. For example,

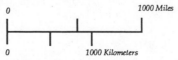

0   1000 Miles

0   1000 Kilometers

A Comparison of Map Scales

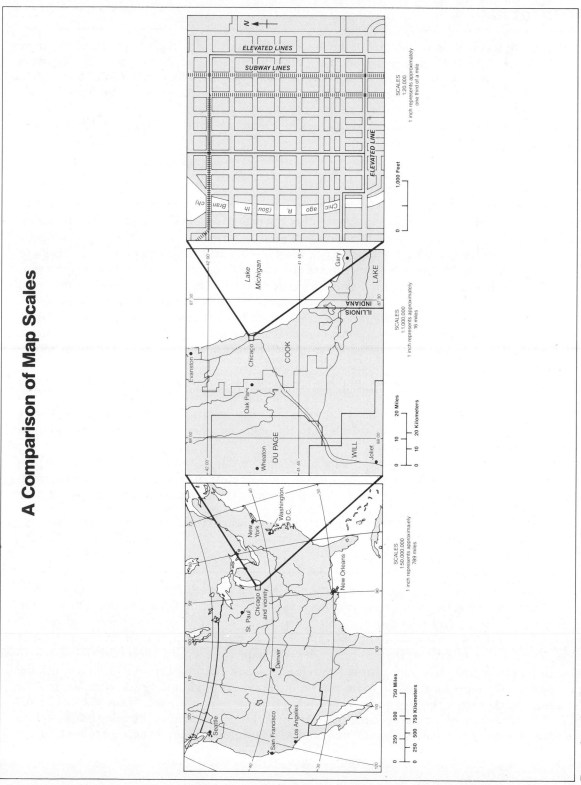

Landforms

Landforms are features on the surface of the land. Elevation refers to a place's distance above or below sea level. The difference in elevation between the highest and lowest points in an area is known as local relief. Generally speaking, sharply rising land with local relief of at least 2,000 feet is called a mountain. A hill rises more or less—the designation is not a precise one—at least 500 feet. A generally flat area that rises far above the surrounding land on at least one side is known as a plateau, or tableland. Land that is nearly level or gently rolling, usually with local relief of less than 500 feet, is called a plain.

Climate and Weather

Climate is essentially accumulated average weather. Weather changes constantly, depending on temperature, moisture, atmospheric pressure, and wind. Over the long term, weather adopts a certain average pattern. Where temperatures are hot to warm and precipitation is heavy to moderate, forests flourish. Where temperatures are warm enough but precipitation is lighter, or where it falls only in one season, a tall-grass prairie develops. Even less precipitation results in the growth of short grasses. In addition to temperature and precipitation, atmospheric pressure, or the weight of the air, significantly influences the character of weather and climate. The standard measure of atmospheric pressure is by barometer. At sea level air pressure is 14.7 pounds per square inch, or, expressed in terms of barometric pressure, 29.92 inches. When air moves from high-pressure areas to low-pressure areas, wind blows.

Wind is also an element in weather, and it affects longer-term climate. It can be thought of as a river of air flowing downhill. Winds that flow continually between global pressure belts are called prevailing winds. These are affected by the force of the earth's rotation. Westerly winds, for example, blow from the subtropical highs to the subpolar lows and tend therefore to blow from the southwest to the northeast.

Weather has an effect on human activities on any given day. Climate has a much more profound long-term impact. The well-watered forest lands of eastern North America and the well-watered central lowlands made possible the development of an agricultural base that would have been very different if aridity had mainly characterized those regions.

Reading a Map

Maps—representations of the earth or a portion of it—can be used for a variety of special purposes. They may reveal a route taken by some person or expedition from one point to another. Or they may show several routes in the same general region. The reader of the map can tell from the key or legend that a solid line or a dotted line or other indicator is showing a particular route. In following the route, the careful reader will note other information that the map provides, such as details of physical features or the cities, states, or nations through or near which the route passes. The direction of the route can be discerned through noting the compass rose or directional marker or, if there is none, by assuming that north is at the top of the map. The distance traveled can be observed by using the scale of miles or kilometers provided. It is well to take note of any special features on the map and to be careful, if several routes intersect, to distinguish among them.

Sometimes a map will have an inset—that is, some portion of the map will be expanded in size to enable the reader to see a representation of one portion of the area enlarged. The enlargement, side by side with the rest of the map, permits simultaneous examination of a smaller and a larger area. An inset is particularly useful in "blowing up" the site of a historical event and at the same time showing the larger geographical context. The reader should be careful to note the difference in scale between the two parts of the map.

Sometimes maps represent matters that are not essentially geographical. A map, for example, that shows the distribution of something over an area is often more interested in the distribution than the area. A map of the state-by-state results of a presidential election may show through the use of symbols or shadings the winner of the electoral vote in each state or, perhaps, the winner of the electoral vote and the proportion of the popular vote. Whenever votes or other activities not essentially geographical are shown, the reader of the map must take care to identify precisely what the map intends to convey. This kind of map can be used to reveal a distribution over a geographic area that cannot be "seen" from a mere chart.

The maps reproduced in this book are instructional tools. After the overview and questions in Part II, the maps become more specific. Use Part II to develop a good grasp of the geographical characteristics of the United States.

The United States: A Geographic and Climatic Portrait

The United States has an area of 3,540,939 square miles, and in 1990 its population was counted at 249,632,692. Its gross national product of more than $4.8 trillion, its per capita annual income of $16,444 (both as of 1988), and its use of more than a third of the world's energy mark it as one of the world's wealthiest nations. The United States is inhabited by a vigorous and productive people who, over the course of their history, developed political and economic structures that unleashed their energy and ingenuity. Easy immigration added to the country's human resources, and widespread education improved the nation. The United States also has benefited from the security of two major ocean boundaries, and no major conflict with neighbors north or south after mid-nineteenth century.

Much of the success of the United States can also be attributed to its great natural wealth. It has extensive deposits of metals and fuels, ample water resources in much of the nation, a wide range of climates and soils, and extensive forests and grasslands. Its river systems and the position of its lowlands were well suited to the development of communication and to the widespread dispersal and settlement of its population. The rivers supplied power as well as transportation, and the ample timber resources of the East provided abundant fuel and building materials.

Driven by self-interest, Europeans moved into the New World and forced back or subordinated the native peoples. In the South the Spanish established themselves on the Caribbean islands, moved into the coastal plain around the Gulf of Mexico, and then on to the high plateau of Mexico and the lands that became the southeastern United States. Farther north and east, the British crossed the Atlantic coastal plain and the Appalachian Mountains and pushed into the vast interior basin of the Great Lakes. The French traveled north beyond the Appalachians, entered the Gulf of St. Lawrence, and, keeping south of the massive Laurentian plateau, moved into the interior, on to the Great Lakes, and then down the Mississippi River to the Gulf of Mexico. In the process, the French took control of the interior heartland. To the west the Russians used the Aleutian Islands to enter Alaska and move down the coast toward the Columbia River. Other explorers doubled Cape Horn at the extremity of South America and traveled up the west coast to the Columbia. Still others journeyed to what is today the U.S. West through the interior of North America, overland and along river routes, and crossed the Rocky Mountains to reach the Columbia River and the Pacific Ocean.

It took two hundred years for the Europeans and then the Americans to learn the major characteristics of their corner of the world. Through a combination of scientific study and practical experience, they learned to understand, use, and exploit the climatic and geological opportunities in their environment. They explored the temperate and humid coastal plain of the

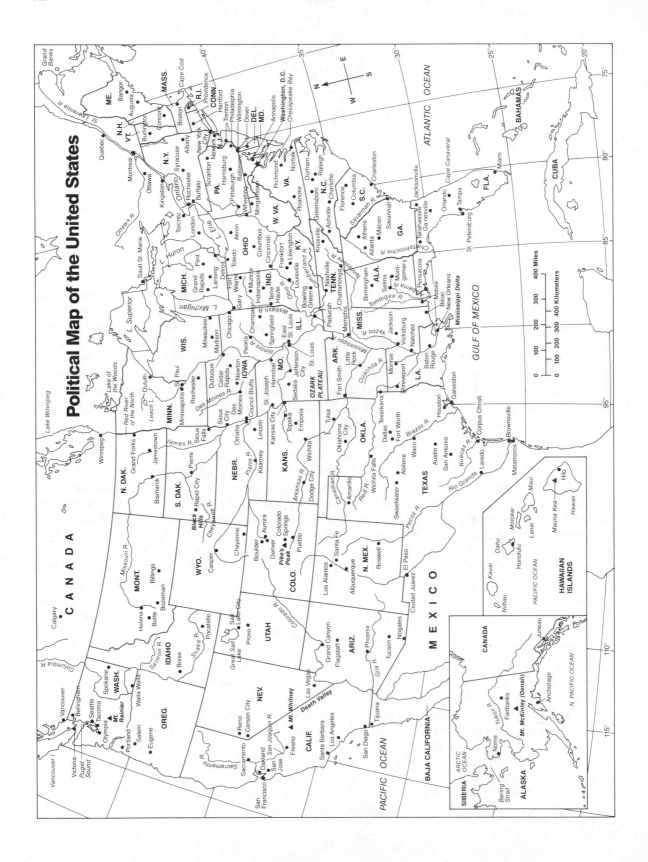

Political Map of the United States

Atlantic and later the central lowlands south of the Great Lakes and in the Ohio and Mississippi valleys. They found that the land offered great opportunities for agriculture. They discovered extensive reserves of timber in the Appalachians, and, later, huge coal fields under them and in the Ohio and central Mississippi basins. Iron deposits lay near the shores of Lake Superior and elsewhere in the lakes region. On the West Coast, lush valleys and ample timber also attracted agriculturalists. And crossing the Great Plains of the western interior, adventurers found non-ferrous metals in the mountains and the intermontane plateaus. They learned that oil and natural gas lay under the Great Plains and the Gulf of Mexico lowlands, in the central basin of California, and in Alaska.

New England

In New England, European settlers often ventured into the region's forested wilderness in groups, sustaining one another and giving communal aid and support, often as members of a single congregation. Although the more adventurous soon moved inland, the coast was the first frontier. The New England shore is characterized by many good but small harbors, their rocky headlands commonly extending to the water's edge. Inland, the mountains of the upland area are geologically old and worn down by erosion. Thus the agricultural land is handicapped by rockiness and poor drainage in large parts of the region. On the other hand, coastal areas have a milder climate than might be expected for the latitude because of the influence of the sea, and the precipitation of 40 to 55 inches is well distributed throughout the year. The early settlers founded several important cities, and commerce formed the major part of the nonagricultural sector of the economy. The port city of Boston soon became the urban center of the region.

The South

In the South, too, the earliest settlements necessarily sprang up along the coast, a region of sandbars and marshes, even though lands in the interior were better drained than on the coast itself. Lacking numbers at first, the settlers imported slaves as a population supplement, one that became increasingly important both economically and culturally. Reliance on slave labor became firmly fixed by the eighteenth century.

The land in southeastern United States is very flat along the coastal plain and slopes gently toward the sea. Many rivers punctuate the surface as they make their way to the coast. To the west rises the piedmont, the hill country that lies between the coastal plain and the Appalachian Mountains. The coastal plain has a humid subtropical climate characterized by heavy rainfall, generally evenly distributed throughout the year, and a long growing season. Cities were fewer in the South than in the North, and Charleston soon became the major commercial center. In both North and South, settlements developed along the fall line, a chain of rapids and small waterfalls formed at the point where rivers descend from the hill country onto the plain. Ocean shipping could not go farther upriver. This hindrance to navigation required the transfer to another means of transportation, but it also provided a source of water power.

The Appalachian highlands extend from the state of New York to central Alabama, where they end at the gulf coastal plain. The fertile, beautiful Shenandoah Valley and many smaller valleys attracted early settlers, but the prairie lands beyond continued to beckon. The settlers forged westward, using such gaps in the Appalachians as the Mohawk and the Cumberland to enter the great central lowlands.

Physiographic Map of the United States

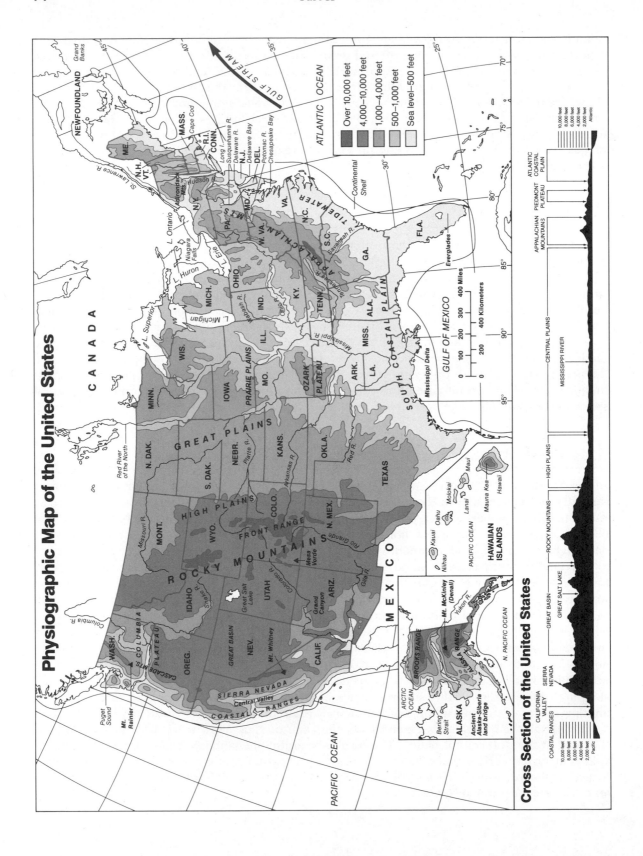

Over 10,000 feet
4,000–10,000 feet
1,000–4,000 feet
500–1,000 feet
Sea level–500 feet

GULF STREAM

ATLANTIC OCEAN

Continental Shelf

TIDEWATER

GULF OF MEXICO

PACIFIC OCEAN

CANADA

MEXICO

0 100 200 300 400 Miles
0 200 400 Kilometers

NEWFOUNDLAND
Grand Banks

ME.
MASS.
Cape Cod
R.I.
CONN.
N.H.
VT.
Long I.
Susquehanna R.
Delaware R.
N.J.
DEL.
Potomac R.
Chesapeake Bay

St. Lawrence R.
Adirondack Mts.
Hudson R.
N.Y.
PA.
MD.
VA.
W. VA.
N.C.
S.C.
GA.
FLA.
Savannah R.
Everglades

L. Ontario
L. Erie
Niagara Falls
L. Huron
L. Michigan
L. Superior
L. Michigan

OHIO
IND.
KY.
TENN.
ALA.
MISS.
LA.
ARK.
Wabash R.
Ohio R.
Tennessee R.

MICH.
WIS.
ILL.
IOWA
MO.
MINN.
PRAIRIE PLAINS
OZARK PLATEAU

APPALACHIAN MTS.
SOUTH COASTAL PLAIN
Mississippi Delta

Red River of the North
N. DAK.
S. DAK.
NEBR.
KANS.
OKLA.
TEXAS
GREAT PLAINS
HIGH PLAINS
Missouri R.
Platte R.
Arkansas R.
Red R.
Rio Grande

MONT.
WYO.
COLO.
N. MEX.
ARIZ.
UTAH
IDAHO
FRONT RANGE
ROCKY MOUNTAINS
Mesa Verde
Colorado R.
Grand Canyon
Gila R.

WASH.
OREG.
NEV.
CALIF.
Great Salt Lake
GREAT BASIN
Mt. Whitney
SIERRA NEVADA
Central Valley
COASTAL RANGES
CASCADE MTS.
COLUMBIA PLATEAU
Columbia R.
Snake R.
Puget Sound
Mt. Rainier

ALASKA
ARCTIC OCEAN
BROOKS RANGE
ALASKA RANGE
Mt. McKinley (Denali)
Yukon R.
Bering Strait
Ancient Alaska-Siberia land bridge
N. PACIFIC OCEAN

HAWAIIAN ISLANDS
Kauai
Niihau
Oahu
Molokai
Lanai
Maui
Hawaii
Mauna Kea
PACIFIC OCEAN

Cross Section of the United States

10,000 feet
8,000 feet
6,000 feet
4,000 feet
2,000 feet
Atlantic

ATLANTIC COASTAL PLAIN
PIEDMONT PLATEAU
APPALACHIAN MOUNTAINS
CENTRAL PLAINS
MISSISSIPPI RIVER
HIGH PLAINS
ROCKY MOUNTAINS
GREAT BASIN
GREAT SALT LAKE
SIERRA NEVADA
CALIFORNIA VALLEY
COASTAL RANGES
Pacific

10,000 feet
8,000 feet
6,000 feet
4,000 feet
2,000 feet
Pacific

The Mississippi River Valley

The Tennessee, Cumberland, and Ohio rivers from the east, and the Illinois, Missouri, and Platte rivers from the west, as well as many others, join the mighty Mississippi to make the Mississippi Valley a fertile plain. Some early New Englanders abandoned the struggle with their region's harsh and unyielding soil and carried their knowledge of raising cattle, poultry, wheat, oats, and hay into the central lowlands. Farther south, some colonists transplanted their tobacco and cotton—and their plantation culture—in the West, to the Mississippi and beyond. The entire Mississippi Valley is characterized by land that is mostly level or gently undulating, with an occasional low hill. The soil is generally fertile, and the climate notable for abrupt seasonal and day-to-day changes in weather conditions. Because there are not significant topographic barriers, the climatic patterns across the region are broad. Temperatures and length of growing season increase more or less uniformly from north to south, and precipitation decreases from east to west. Fertile soils and humid climate make this region the nation's agricultural heartland. Cities grew up at the commercial nodes along the rivers. New Orleans was premier among them, but upriver, settlers founded Memphis, St. Louis, Louisville, and Cincinnati. Although Chicago got a late start, its position on Lake Michigan and its rise as a railroad center after mid-nineteenth century paved the way for its phenomenal growth.

The West

West of the Missouri River, pioneers found the geographical situation much changed. Some passed through and pressed on over the mountains to Oregon in the 1840s. Those who stopped, however, found that west of the Missouri River, humidity gave way to aridity. There the land was no longer forest or moist prairie with wood for building and for fuel. The soil is extremely fertile in most places—with exceptions like the Nebraska sand hills—but the semiarid conditions deteriorated in very dry years to near-desert conditions. Winters are extremely cold and dry, summers very hot and dry, and the brisk winds of the flat countryside tend to speed evaporation. Migrants at the leading edge of settlement had to choose: they could learn to live in these short-grass plains and arid basins; they could turn back; or they could proceed farther west. Those who stayed developed the cattle and sheep empires of the plains, in the process virtually eliminating the buffalo and antelope herds. Soon enough, however, farmers followed the ranchers and fenced the plains, and by using dry-farming methods, they took over the subhumid range and established the nation's bountiful spring and winter wheat belts.

The fertile Willamette Valley brought settlers to the Oregon country. From there, some went south to California. It was the rush for gold in 1849 that provided the major stimulus for the large California migration, but in its aftermath the great central valley of the Sacramento and the San Joaquin rivers, lying between the Sierra Nevada and the coast ranges, became a center of agricultural production. Large-scale lumbering was not far behind. San Francisco, with its excellent harbor, soon dominated as the regional metropolis.

Those intent on their rush to the coast bypassed the Rocky Mountains and the intermontane region, the land between the Rockies and the Sierra Nevada of California and the Cascade Mountains farther north. But soon the seekers of precious metals began returning eastward to the mountains. There, after prospectors unearthed dazzling mineral deposits, boom towns swiftly sprang up in remote valleys and gulches. The population rose sharply, and some stayed even after the mining rushes had passed. As the western mountains became the scene of giant lumbering and logging enterprises, mining remained a part of the regional economic scene.

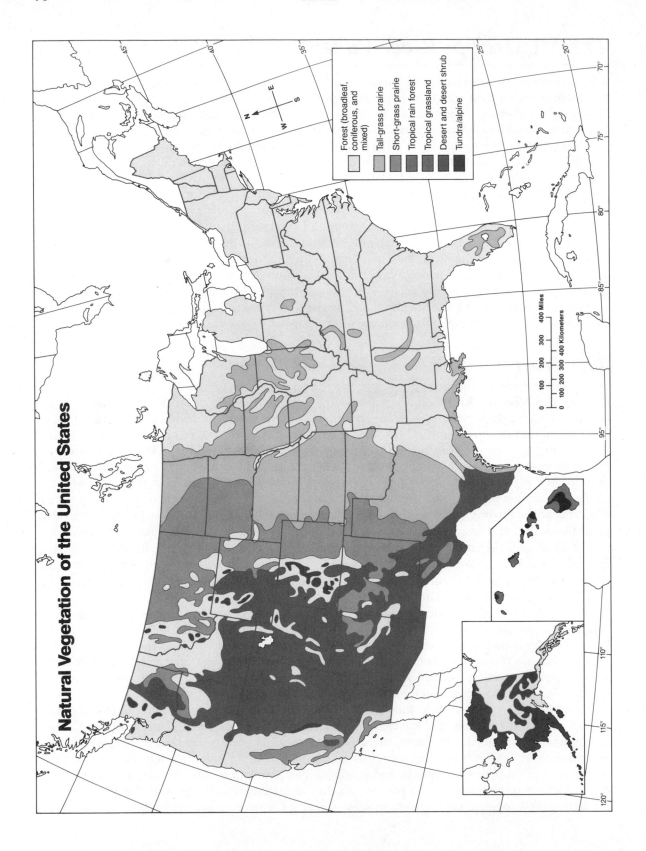

Natural Vegetation of the United States

Forest (broadleaf, coniferous, and mixed)
Tall-grass prairie
Short-grass prairie
Tropical rain forest
Tropical grassland
Desert and desert shrub
Tundra/alpine

Stock raising and farming also developed, and irrigation agriculture was established in the dry regions to the south.

Climate

The United States is generally characterized by cold winters, hot summers, rapidly changing weather conditions, and strong contrasts between dry and humid areas. All result from the continent's position, size, shape, and relief. Much of northern United States has significantly cold winters as a result of the size and extent of the continental land mass. Such land masses lose their heat quickly in winter. In North America a powerful continental polar air mass dominates the greater part of the continent. In the summer the central lowlands heat up far more than do oceans at the same latitude. When low-pressure systems develop, they pull tropical air from the Gulf of Mexico right up to the Great Lakes. Because the same areas cool down to freezing temperatures in winter, a climate of extremes characterizes the region. On the West Coast humid conditions spawned by a maritime Pacific air mass rapidly give way to dry conditions in the intermontane basins as air moving westward dumps its moisture west of the mountains. A broad belt of arid or semiarid climate runs up the continent's western interior. On the East Coast the maritime Atlantic air mass has only a slightly moderating influence. Continental conditions spread over eastern United States well into the Atlantic coastal plain.

The forty-eight contiguous continental states of the United States lie between 24° and 49° north latitude and between 66° and 125° west longitude. Beyond the contiguous forty-eight, the Union includes the massive state of Alaska to the north, notable for its mineral wealth, its arresting physical beauty, and the harsh subarctic character of its interior. Its southern coast and the Alaskan panhandle provide plentiful agricultural and forest resources. Alaska's easternmost point lies at almost 130° west longitude, and the state extends into the Eastern Hemisphere, where the westernmost of the Aleutian Islands is at 172° east longitude. From south to north, Alaska lies between 54° and 72° north latitude. The United States also includes the sunkissed Hawaiian Islands in the Pacific Ocean, situated in a tropical fringe location. The Union's fiftieth state extends from south of 19° to north of 25° north latitude. From west to east it stretches from 176° west longitude almost to 155°. The rich agricultural lands it boasts today were the lure that brought planters to Hawaii in the nineteenth century. Hawaii's location as a naval station was and remains of great importance to the nation.

These, then, are the major characteristics of the United States. The maps on the preceding pages permit you to survey several aspects of the nation as a whole—its political divisions and its physical features. As you proceed through the narrative and exercises in Part III, you will examine the nation's growth and development in greater detail. The maps provided in Part III will clarify where and how that growth and development took place. They will show where history happened.

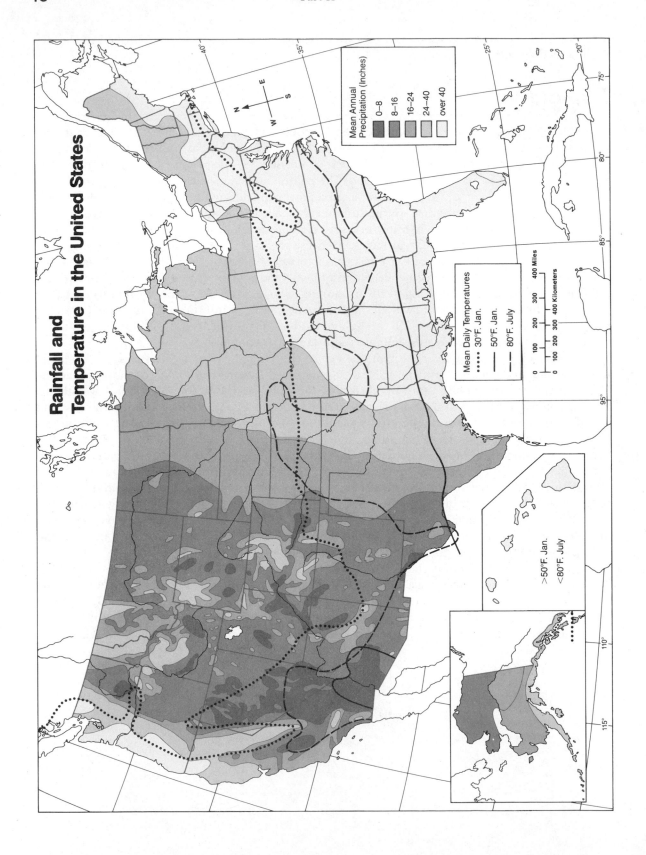

Rainfall and Temperature in the United States

Mean Annual Precipitation (Inches)
0–8
8–16
16–24
24–40
over 40

Mean Daily Temperatures
30°F. Jan.
50°F. Jan.
80°F. July

400 Miles
0   100 200 300 400 Kilometers

>50°F. Jan.
<80°F. July

Political Map of the United States

1. On the map, label the location of your college or university. Mark off a radius of 500 miles around it. Name and underline the states or portions of states and the cities that are included in the circle. Do the same for mountains and rivers.

2. Mark off a 500-mile radius around Billings, Montana; Pittsburgh, Pennsylvania; Birmingham, Alabama; Albuquerque, New Mexico; Tulsa, Oklahoma; Sioux City, Iowa; and Memphis, Tennessee. Name and underline the states or portions of states, the cities, and the rivers and mountains that are included in the circles.

3. Do the same for your home town if you have not already done so in answer to question 1 or 2.

4. Learn to recognize all 50 states by their shape in relation to the shapes of surrounding states.

5. Can you name all the state capitals?

Physiographic Map of the United States

The objective is to learn the regions.

1. Name the states or portions of states in the south coastal plain.
2. Name the states or portions of states in the Atlantic coastal plain, called the tidewater.
3. Name the states or portions of states in the piedmont.
4. Name the states or portions of states in the Appalachian Mountains.
5. Name the states or portions of states in the central plains or lowlands, comprising the prairie plains and the lower Mississippi Valley.
6. Name the states or portions of states in the Great Plains and high plains.
7. Name the states or portions of states in the Rocky Mountains.
8. What states or portions of states lie in the intermontane region?

Natural Vegetation of the United States

The objective is to learn the regions.

1. Name the states or portions of states in the eastern forest region.
2. Name the states or portions of states in the tall-grass prairie.
3. Name the states or portions of states in the short-grass prairie.
4. Name the states or portions of states in the desert and desert-shrub region.
5. Name the states or portions of states in the western forest region.

Rainfall and Temperature in the United States

1. Trace the line in the plains region that shows the eastern edge of the area of less than 16 inches of annual average rainfall. Through which states does it pass? What is the approximate line of longitude?

2. Trace the line showing an average January temperature of 30°F. Through which states does it pass? Why does it turn so sharply north at its western extremity?

Some Additional Points

1. Note the limits of latitude and longitude for the United States, including Alaska and Hawaii. Mark them on the political map.

2. For the location of your college or university, mark the latitude and longitude.

3. For the location of your home, mark the latitude and longitude.

Part III

Exercises

Unit 1

Voyages of Discovery

Born in Genoa, probably in 1451, Christopher Columbus was a young man of about twenty-five when he was shipwrecked off the coast of Portugal. For the next several years he made a number of voyages from his home in that land or from the island of Madeira. During these years of involvement in Portugal, the "Enterprise of the Indies" took shape in Columbus's thinking. If the Portuguese could sail so far south—and they were going farther into unknown waters along the coast of Africa year by year—it should surely be possible to sail as far to the west.

By the late fifteenth century no reasonable person believed that the earth was flat. Columbus was not unique in that respect. Certainly sailors who had seen the hulls of ships vanish below the horizon knew that the earth was curved. The question, however, was this: in traveling west might one go so far as never to be able to get back? Columbus was ready to contemplate so hazardous a voyage because the European demand for the spices and luxuries of the East was ever growing. Wealth and honor awaited those who were daring enough to venture directly to the East without the arduous, dangerous, and expensive journey through the eastern Mediterranean and across Asia. That meant going west. A forward-looking monarch should be able to see as much, Columbus concluded. He therefore took his proposition to King João II of Portugal, who quite reasonably rejected it. The distance was too great for seafarers safely to undertake such a voyage.

Columbus moved on to Spain. Until 1492 King Ferdinand and Queen Isabella of Spain were fully occupied with reconquering the peninsula from the Moors. Nevertheless, Columbus was subsidized from the royal purse while his great enterprise was in abeyance. The members of the royal commission appointed to consider Columbus's proposal finally rejected it, not because they thought that the earth was flat but because they too believed that the distance was too great. Once Spanish victory against the Moors was assured, however, Isabella accepted the risk. Columbus and his fleet of three ships sailed from Palos bound for the Canary Islands. On September 6 the ships left the Canaries and, with the trade winds at their backs, sailed west. By the end of September, the crew were getting worried. With the wind constantly from the east, would they ever get back? By cajolery, aggressiveness, and false bookkeeping, Columbus persuaded his men to carry on. They made landfall on October 12 at Guanahaní, which Columbus renamed San Salvador. Historians consider two islands in the present-day Bahamas group possible sites of the historic landing.

Celestial navigation—plotting a position on the earth's surface through observation of the heavenly bodies—was in its infancy in Columbus's time. Columbus based his navigation on dead reckoning, at which he was a master. He laid out his course and set and maintained the ship's direction by the compass heading. He determined his rate of speed by a chip log, a wooden weight attached to a line in which knots were spaced so that the number of knots paid out over the rail in a half-minute measured the rate of forward progress. Passage of time was determined by the ship's clock, a half-hour glass containing enough sand to run from the upper to the lower section in precisely thirty minutes, to be quickly turned over. The ship's rate of speed and the passage of time determined how far along their course each day's journey brought the mariners. Adding to the possibilities of error inherent in such a method, a calculating Columbus deceived his sailors about the distance traveled, to allay their apprehensions. Ironically, he greatly overestimated the distance. The propagandized record that he revealed to his sailors was more nearly accurate than his own private log.

In 1493 and 1494 a papal bull and a treaty between Portugal and Spain assured Spain of title to all of the Western Hemisphere 370 leagues west of the Cape Verde Islands. Inspired by Columbus's initial success, Henry VII of England ignored the treaty and supported the expedition of another Genoese explorer, Giovanni Caboto, known as John Cabot, in a search for a route to the East. Cabot's expedition in 1497 was the first to touch North America since the Viking voyages. In contrast with Spain, however, England did nothing for the next fifty years to develop its claim to North America. England was content to profit from its European wool trade and, with the exception of fishing, to leave America alone.

France's interest in America also developed slowly. After a French privateer captured a Spanish ship carrying bullion from Mexico, Francis I sent the Florentine Giovanni Verrazano to North America. Verrazano claimed for France much of what is now the East Coast of the United States. The pope reprimanded Francis, pointing out that all non-Christian lands had been divided between Portugal and Spain. Francis responded by asking sarcastically to see "the will of our father Adam" that disposed of the earth in such a fashion.

Spain enjoyed a near monopoly in the New World for almost a hundred years. It was Spain's *siglo de oro*, its golden age. England and France looked enviously at the flow of riches from Mexico and Peru to Spain. Throughout most of the sixteenth century, however, no nation was able or willing to challenge Spanish power.

A. Map Exercises

1. Both King Joao II of Portugal and, at first, Isabella of Spain refused help to Columbus because they regarded the distance to the East to be too great. Columbus estimated about 2,800 statute miles to Japan. Using the map, estimate the actual distance between Palos, Spain, and the Canary Islands and then from the Canaries to Guanahaní. If America had not stood in the way, what might have been Columbus's fate?

2. The treaty between Spain and Portugal placed the dividing line in the New World 370 leagues west of the Cape Verde Islands. Locate these islands on the map, southwest of the Canaries. Make an estimate of the location of that dividing line, assuming three miles to the league, and draw a north-south line. Through which present-day countries does it pass? This line is unlikely to coincide with major present national boundaries. Imperial ambition ultimately swept over the treaty that had been made.

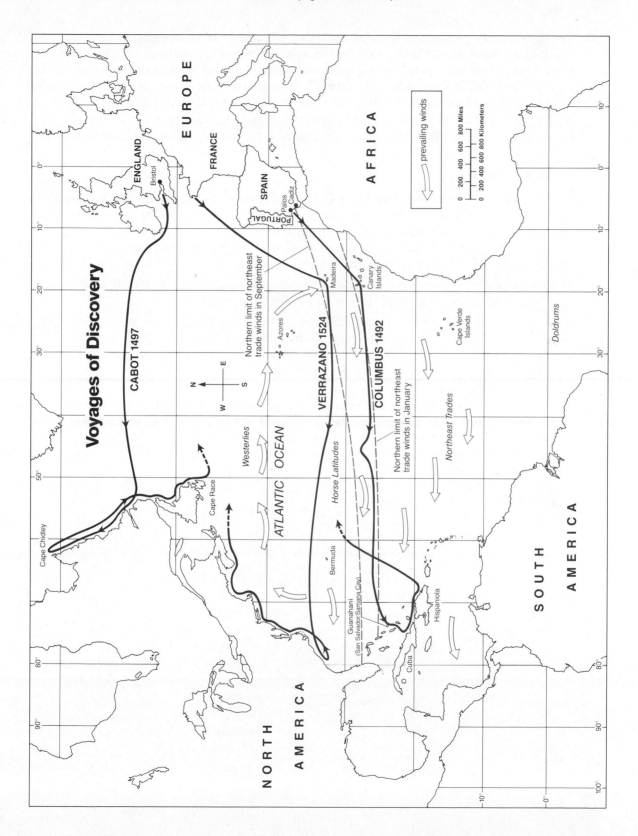

Voyages of Discovery

CABOT 1497

VERRAZANO 1524

COLUMBUS 1492

EUROPE

ENGLAND
Bristol

FRANCE

SPAIN
PORTUGAL
Palos
Cadiz

AFRICA

prevailing winds

0 200 400 600 800 Miles
0 200 400 600 800 Kilometers

Madeira
Canary
Islands

Cape Verde
Islands

Doldrums

Northern limit of northeast
trade winds in September

Azores

N
E
W · S

Westerlies

ATLANTIC OCEAN

Horse Latitudes

Northern limit of northeast
trade winds in January

Northeast Trades

Cape Race

Cape Chidley

NORTH
AMERICA

Bermuda

Guanahani
(San Salvador/Samana Cay)

Cuba

Hispaniola

SOUTH
AMERICA

3. The Azores were Portuguese as the Canaries were Spanish. If Columbus had sailed for Portugal, he probably would have made for the Azores as a first landfall and then set out to the west. Look at the wind patterns of a route due west from the Azores. Compare them to the wind patterns of the route actually taken, due west from the Canaries. How successful would Columbus have been if he had sailed for Portugal instead of Spain?

4. John Cabot crossed the Atlantic later and farther north than did Columbus. On the map label the lands along which he coasted. Do the same for the voyage of Giovanni Verrazano.

B. Further Exercises

1. The November 1986 issue of the *National Geographic* magazine devotes a special section to "Columbus and the New World." The authors urge acceptance of Samana Cay rather than San Salvador as the true landing site of the navigator. They contend that earlier estimates of Columbus's route did not take adequate account of "drift" from the true path. Read the article. Write a brief essay giving your view.

2. The major port of embarkation on the southern Spanish coast in the latter fifteenth century was Cadiz. Yet Columbus's little fleet put out from Palos. Why?

3. Although Columbus's name in its English or Spanish version (Colón) is found in many places in the New World, the continents themselves are not named after him. Someone else has gained that honor. Do some research into who this individual was, and write a brief biographical sketch of the person, including the reasons why the Americas bear his name.

4. The map shows three of the many voyages of exploration undertaken in the fifteenth and sixteenth centuries. For a long time the New World was considered merely an obstacle to penetration to the East. Can a water route from Europe to the East be found by going west? Describe the route. Who was the first explorer to reach the Pacific Ocean by traversing this route?

Unit 2

North America in Mid-Eighteenth Century

By the middle of the eighteenth century, what would happen in North America and to its aboriginal inhabitants lay in the hands of Spain, France, and Great Britain. These nations had different goals and purposes, and these were reflected in the way they settled and used the land and its resources.

Spain had been the first foreign nation to make a foothold in the New World. Its original search for a route to the East turned within a short time to exploitation of the Caribbean islands and South and Central America for gold and silver. In the sixteenth century the Spanish presence in Mexico and the Caribbean was extended northward by explorations in Florida, in the Mississippi-Arkansas region, and in what is now the Southwest of the United States. By the eighteenth century the Spanish had established forts, trading bases, and Catholic missions in Florida and the Southwest. Spanish settlement was never dense in these areas, but the presence of Spain was always significant.

France made several early efforts to establish itself in the New World. It was not until the beginning of the seventeenth century, however, that French attempts to colonize Canada took root, with a settlement at Port Royal in Acadia (later Nova Scotia) and another at Quebec, later to become the capital of New France. Fishing and fur trading were the people's principal economic pursuits. The holders of the fur monopoly were not eager for any sizable immigration to the colony that might drive out fur-bearing animals, and by midcentury perhaps only 400 French colonists lived in New France. Later, Louis XIV saw the New World as a source of strength to support French glory in Europe. New France's timber would supply the navy, and the fur trade would be developed to bring gold to the treasury. New France grew in population. The Mississippi and Missouri rivers were explored. The military and the Church began building forts and missions throughout the Great Lakes region and the Mississippi Valley. France laid claim to the drainage basin of the entire Mississippi River and all the rivers that fed it. By mid-eighteenth century France achieved its ambition of connecting Canada and Louisiana by a chain of forts and trading posts. The French and the English clashed three times in wars fought both in Europe and in North America. During these years France learned to exploit more effectively than the English the military talents of their Indian allies.

The British colonies on the North American mainland were established, after some initial failures, between 1607 and 1732. Using a variety of techniques ranging from settlement by an advance agent who assumed all risk to settlement under direct royal control, the British established thirteen continental colonies. They actively encouraged settlement and achieved a population of more than a million by mid-eighteenth century. Efforts by such European nations as the Netherlands and Sweden to establish colonies where the English wished control were beaten back. It was the French in the interior and the Spanish to the south that concerned the British.

The greatest number of settlers in the British colonies were English people who came for economic and religious reasons. Yeoman farmers and hardworking merchants were well represented among the migrants. Landowners recently risen from the yeoman class were also present. Many were literate, even though the number of aristocrats was small. The English settlers tended to be a hardworking, energetic lot.

German settlers were numerous. A series of wars wracked the German states in the seventeenth and eighteenth centuries. Taxes, political instability, and religious intolerance drove thousands of Germans to leave the Rhineland, the Palatinate, and other areas, and to make the long journey to America. They settled first near Philadelphia and then elsewhere in Pennsylvania and New Jersey. Many went to the Mohawk Valley of New York. Others traveled down the Appalachian front to the Cumberland Valley of Maryland and Virginia and then out through the Shenandoah Valley to the frontier of North Carolina. As with most non-English-speaking immigrants, especially those with distinctive religious views, the Germans tended to keep to themselves. Relations between them and the English were not always cordial.

During the seventeenth century several English governments had moved to establish firmer control in Ireland, to the disadvantage of the Irish. Protestants were introduced into Ulster in northern Ireland; they were Presbyterians from the Scottish Lowlands who proceeded to prosper, only to be thwarted by English restrictions against their goods. To add to their distress, a series of famines struck in the eighteenth century. Many of the Scotch-Irish—the Protestants of Ulster—sought new opportunities in America. By 1730 the Cumberland and Shenandoah valleys were filling up with Scotch-Irish farmers. The settlement pattern stretched south to the Carolinas and then east from the mountains, to populate the piedmont. Soon the region was characterized by English settlements in the east and Scotch-Irish and Germans to the west. Like the Germans, the Scotch-Irish settled in separate communities. They felt as little affection for the Anglican English as they had for the Catholic Irish.

Immigration to British America by Africans was involuntary. Although the legal character of chattel slavery in the British colonies was only beginning to become clear by the end of the seventeenth century, substantial numbers of Africans had already been brought to America. Most North American slaves had come from the agricultural tribes of West Africa. Though nonliterate, the Africans had grown up in social and political structures of some complexity. Their lives had revolved around an extended family with strong kinship loyalties. The economies of West Africa tended to be stable, with property held in common for use by family groups. The culture shock experienced by slaves was obviously more severe than for any other group. They lost their freedom, their kinship group, and to some degree two essential elements of their culture when they were forced to learn English and to adopt the religious inclinations of their masters.

Native American societies in North America had great variety. It was the eastern woodland Indians with whom the English and the French came into contact. Both nations were convinced of their own religious and moral superiority. The English often rationalized their assaults on the Indians by denying that they were worthy of any human consideration. The French were more accepting, but they too wished to subordinate the Indian peoples, and they won the unending enmity of the Iroquois. In Virginia and North Carolina Algonquian-speaking tribes, and in New England the Narragansetts, the Wampanoags, and the Pequots, were pushed back or destroyed by the settlers. Both France and England wanted the Ohio Valley. The Indians were caught in the middle.

At the middle of the eighteenth century, the three European empires of France, Great Britain, and Spain in North America were poised for conflict. These nations expected settlers of other nationalities to do their part. Depending on their circumstances, the colonists saw Indians as either allies, enemies, or obstacles.

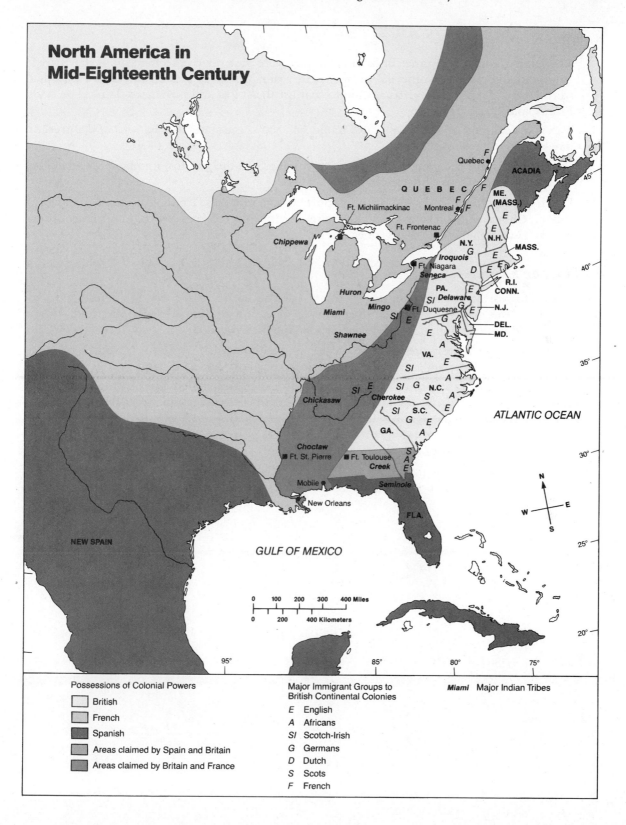

North America in Mid-Eighteenth Century

Quebec ● F

ACADIA

Q U E B E C F

Ft. Michilimackinac

Montreal ● F

ME.
(MASS.)

E

N.H.

MASS.

Chippewa

Ft. Frontenac

N.Y.

G

E

Iroquois

Ft. Niagara

Seneca

D

E

E

R.I.

CONN.

Huron

PA.

E

Delaware

SI

N.J.

Miami

Mingo

Ft. Duquesne

SI

G

DEL.

Shawnee

E

MD.

A

VA.

E

SI

E

Chickasaw

SI

E

SI

G

N.C.

A

Cherokee

S

A

SI

S.C.

E

SI

G

A

GA.

E

Choctaw

S

Creek

A

Ft. St. Pierre

Ft. Toulouse

E

Mobile ●

Seminole

New Orleans

FLA.

ATLANTIC OCEAN

NEW SPAIN

GULF OF MEXICO

N

W ● E

S

45°

40°

35°

30°

25°

20°

0   100   200   300   400 Miles

0   200   400 Kilometers

95°   85°   80°   75°

Possessions of Colonial Powers	Major Immigrant Groups to British Continental Colonies	*Miami* Major Indian Tribes
☐ British	E English	
☐ French	A Africans	
■ Spanish	SI Scotch-Irish	
■ Areas claimed by Spain and Britain	G Germans	
■ Areas claimed by Britain and France	D Dutch	
	S Scots	
	F French	

A. Map Exercises

1. The lands claimed by France in North America were vast relative to the size of the British continental colonies. Name the present states and provinces located in the regions that were New France and Louisiana. Add to that list the states and provinces claimed by both France and Great Britain.

2. The lands claimed by Spain were also immense. Name the states and nations of the present day located in those lands.

3. From a perusal of the map, which colony or colonies had the greatest numbers of Germans? Scotch-Irish? Africans? Scots? Dutch?

4. Learn the locations of several of the important Indian tribes: Iroquois, Seneca, Delaware, Miami, Cherokee, Chickasaw, Creek, Seminole. In what colonies (or states of the contemporary United States) did these tribes dwell?

B. Further Exercises

1. Claims to North American lands were often based on earlier explorations. Investigate and sketch on the map the seventeenth-century exploration routes of Louis Joliet and Father Jacques Marquette and of René Robert de La Salle for France.

2. In like fashion, investigate and sketch the sixteenth-century exploration routes of Juan Ponce de León, Hernando de Soto, and Francisco de Coronado for Spain.

3. In many instances the Scotch-Irish who settled in the southern colonies in the eighteenth century moved east from the mountains to the piedmont rather than west from the coast. What is meant by the word *piedmont*? Settlement patterns in the piedmont were also strongly affected by the extent of the tidewater region and the location of the fall line. Explain these two concepts.

4. Movements south through the mountains from the middle colonies often went through the Cumberland Valley and the Shenandoah Valley. Locate and mark these areas on the map.

Unit 3

North America After the Seven Years' War

In the eighteenth century France, Spain, and Great Britain struggled for power not only on the continent of Europe but in North America as well. Spain maintained a strong grip on Florida and the Gulf Coast as well as in the far west. France had claims in Canada and in the valleys of the Mississippi and Ohio rivers. Great Britain claimed land beyond the Appalachian Mountains and was firmly settled on the Atlantic seaboard from Massachusetts to Georgia. These European powers all had interests in the Caribbean.

From 1739 to 1742, in the so-called War of Jenkins' Ear, Great Britain fought with Spain over trading rights in Caribbean and Central American ports. Georgians, South Carolinians, and Virginians participated in the earliest fighting and made up a majority of those who joined an unsuccessful expedition against Florida and, later, a disastrous failure as far away as the coast of Colombia.

From 1740 to 1748 Britain and France contended in the War of the Austrian Succession, known in America as King George's War. Fought for dynastic and imperial reasons, the war settled little. Even though New Englanders won a glorious victory at the great French fortress of Louisbourg on Cape Breton Island, the fort was returned when the war ended.

Earlier, in 1682, a French expedition reached the mouth of the Mississippi River and claimed the whole region for the grand monarch Louis XIV, the Sun King. But France, more caught up in European affairs than in American ventures, did not actively encourage settlement in its new North American territory. By 1760 no more than 75,000 French subjects lived in all of Canada and the Mississippi Valley, most of them engaged in the fur trade. Because the French were few in number, native Americans were not especially concerned about losing tribal lands to them, who, generally speaking, treated native Americans with respect.

By 1753 the British ministry was aware that France had determined to move into western Pennsylvania and the Ohio Valley for the purpose of taking complete control of the area fur trade. Their intention was to establish themselves at the point where the Allegheny and Monongahela rivers join to form the Ohio. The French move threatened to throw into disarray the plans of the recently formed Ohio Company, made up principally of Virginia land speculators. The Virginia colony sent a young militia officer, one George Washington, to ask the French to depart. They refused. Rather, they strengthened Fort Duquesne at the junction of the three rivers.

Although Great Britain and France remained at peace, the threat of war loomed. The Anglo-French tensions led ten of the British colonies to meet at Albany, New York, in 1754 to discuss the possible formation of a permanent intercolonial union. The Albany Congress accepted Pennsylvania delegate Benjamin Franklin's plan of union, but the colonial assemblies later either rejected or ignored it. In Virginia, the governor called on the mother country to protect Virginia's interests in the Ohio Valley, and in response England dispatched General Edward Braddock to lead a combined British-colonial force to Fort Duquesne. Braddock suffered an inglorious defeat at the hands of a mixed force of French and Indians near the fort. Fighting had begun, and formal war was soon to follow. Fear that France might try to regain Acadia (Nova Scotia) led the British government in 1755 to deport—with unnecessary cruelty—several thousand French inhabitants from the area.

The Seven Years' War (1756—1763) was known in America as the French and Indian War. It was unmistakably a war for empire. William Pitt, the king's chief minister, let Britain's ally Prussia bear the burden of the war in Europe while he placed much of England's military might in America. His purpose was to strangle New France, and he succeeded.

At the Peace of Paris in 1763, the British redrew the map of North America. Great Britain took Florida from Spain and Canada from France. Spain's compensations were New Orleans and the lands west of the Mississippi, which France had unwisely promised to Spain for its entry into the war in 1762. Except for St. Domingue and several smaller islands in the Caribbean, St. Pierre and Miquelon off the Canadian coast, and certain fishing rights, France was effectively banished as British sovereignty extended from Canada to the Mississippi.

British arms had triumphed not only in America and Europe but also in Asia and Africa, and at sea. In the process, however, Britain acquired a huge debt. Dealing with this heavy burden set in motion a series of events, including the imposition of taxes and other revenue-raising measures, that significantly intensified the friction between Americans and English. Although Americans reveled in their victory and felt relief from the threat of French and Spanish provocation of Indian attacks on the frontiers, at the same time they became apprehensive about the presence of a large standing army. Moreover, they came away from their experience of war without a need to be supervised by authorities from overseas and a growing sense of American identity.

A. Map Exercises

1. One of the earliest battles in the French and Indian War occurred well before war broke out in Europe. Braddock's defeat took place at Fort Duquesne, situated where the Allegheny and Monongahela rivers join to form the Ohio. The Ohio River is marked on the map. Draw in the other two rivers and label Fort Duquesne, now Pittsburgh.

2. One of the great battles of the war was fought in 1759 when British general Wolfe defeated French general Montcalm on the Plains of Abraham just outside Quebec. On the map, label both Quebec and the river that the city overlooks.

3. The map shows the Proclamation Line of 1763 clearly and neatly. The line was, however, notably porous and uncertain. Why was it drawn? And why was it porous and uncertain?

4. The map shows the thirteen continental British colonies without naming them individually. They should be easily identifiable. Label them.

5. Although Russia claimed lands in North America in the 1750s, its holdings were so far distant from those of the French and the British that these nations paid Russia little attention. From the map, estimate the distance from the Russian claims to Fort Duquesne.

6. Like Quebec and Fort Duquesne, Albany is another city on a river. Label the city and draw in and label its river.

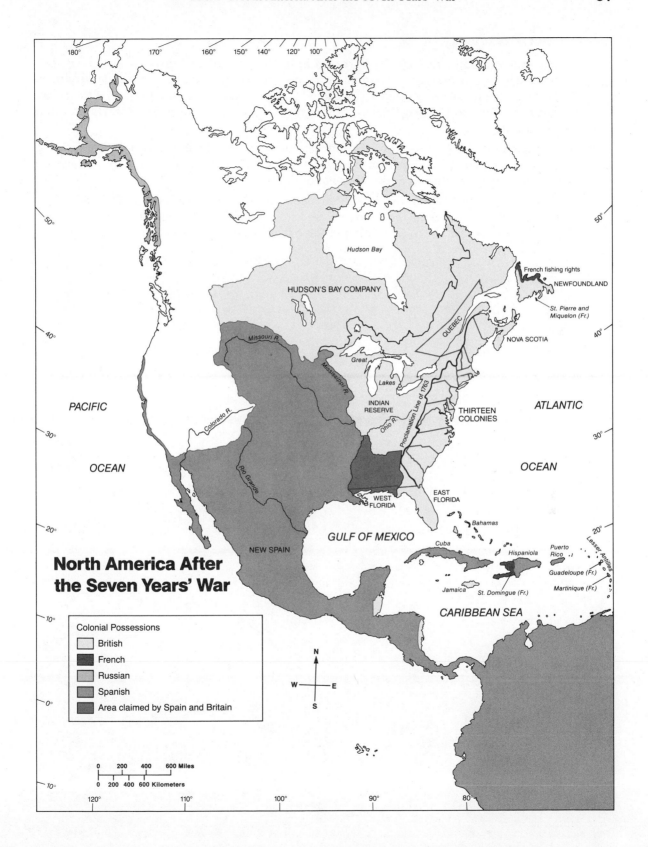

North America After the Seven Years' War

Colonial Possessions

- British
- French
- Russian
- Spanish
- Area claimed by Spain and Britain

HUDSON'S BAY COMPANY

Hudson Bay

French fishing rights

NEWFOUNDLAND

St. Pierre and Miquelon (Fr.)

QUEBEC

NOVA SCOTIA

Missouri R.

Mississippi R.

Great

Lakes

INDIAN
RESERVE

Ohio R.

Proclamation Line of 1763

THIRTEEN
COLONIES

Colorado R.

Rio Grande

PACIFIC

OCEAN

ATLANTIC

OCEAN

WEST
FLORIDA

EAST
FLORIDA

NEW SPAIN

GULF OF MEXICO

Bahamas

Cuba

Hispaniola

*Puerto
Rico*

Guadeloupe (Fr.)

Jamaica

St. Domingue (Fr.)

Martinique (Fr.)

Lesser Antilles

CARIBBEAN SEA

N
W E
S

0   200   400   600 Miles

0   200   400   600 Kilometers

B. Further Exercises

1. In 1755 the Acadians were cruelly uprooted from Nova Scotia and dispersed by the British. After much travail and misery, some Acadians settled in what is present-day southern Louisiana. Their name, "Acadians," became "Cajuns." Look into the history of their travels. Write a one- to two-page description of their history and migration. Mark the Cajun region on the map.

2. The map shows the presence of four European powers in North America and the islands. Other nations also claimed territories in North America. Research the matter, and use the map to note the presence of these other nations.

3. Europeans knew little about the North American interior from south of the Colorado River to the far north. However, they had explored some coastal areas. Label present-day Seattle and Vancouver on the West Coast and Cape Breton Island in the east.

Unit 4

The American Revolution

Tensions between Americans and the mother country had been rising since 1763 as Great Britain attempted to strengthen its control over the American colonies. By the mid-1770s attitudes had hardened. The British resolved to meet disobedience with force, and the Americans resolved to resist.

General Thomas Gage, sitting in the governor's chair in Massachusetts, knew from his informants that colonial militia were assembling military supplies at strategic locations. He also learned that Massachusetts was about to send delegates to other New England colonies to discuss the formation of an army. He determined to act, and his preparations alerted patriot leaders. They expected an attempt to capture Samuel Adams and John Hancock, the most outspoken revolutionaries in the colony, and a strike against the supplies at Concord (pronounced Con' kerd in Massachusetts). In the evening of April 18, 1775, Paul Revere and William Dawes left Boston to warn Adams and Hancock, who were hiding in Lexington, and to alert the people of the countryside that the British were coming.

A force of 700 British regulars started out in the darkness of early morning on April 19, bound for Concord. American alarm bells and signal guns indicated that their mission was no secret. At Lexington, colonial militiamen were drawn up on the village green. As the two forces faced each other, a shot of unknown origin rang out, and within the next few minutes the first blood of the Revolution was spilled. The troops resumed their march and reached Concord by 8:00 A.M. The Americans had already removed most of the military stores, but the British found and burned some gun carriages. Alarmed by the sight of smoke rising from the village, colonials stationed some distance away at Concord's North Bridge engaged in another skirmish with the regulars.

At midday the British troops started back to Boston. Colonial militiamen from miles around now awaited their passage. Some 3,000 Americans or more, shooting from behind trees, rocks, and stone walls along the way, poured fire on the 700 regulars, who were joined by 900 reinforcements at Lexington as they retreated toward Boston. Casualties from the "battles" of Lexington and Concord were not high. The British counted 73 killed, 192 wounded, and 22 captured; the Americans, 49 killed and 39 wounded. Now, however, there was no turning back. A long and grueling war had begun.

The British recognized slowly that it was not Massachusetts alone against which they were engaged, but all America. The war began in the North, but within a year the center of fighting shifted to the middle states. After 1779 the major theater moved to the South. In March 1776 the British evacuated Boston, where the absence of loyalist strength and the presence of strategically placed American cannon were worrisome. On the other hand, New York City was more centrally located; it commanded the Hudson River, a major water route into the interior with access to the grain and livestock; and strong loyalist sentiment flourished in the city. For the next two years, the war swept back and forth across New Jersey, Pennsylvania, and New York. In September 1777 the British took Philadelphia, but in October the Americans defeated General John Burgoyne at Saratoga, New York, a major turning point in American fortunes. The French now saw a possible American victory in the war and lent their support.

When the British were unable to win decisively in the middle states, they began a southern campaign. Early success in the coastal areas of Georgia, South Carolina, and North Carolina led nowhere. The British had difficulty advancing their control into the interior. The distances were great, the problem of supply serious, and the reliability of the loyalists uncertain. In 1781, after several losses, the British moved into Virginia, a supply and staging area for the Americans. After initial success, they were pinned down at Yorktown between an American force on land and a French fleet in Chesapeake Bay. The surrender of Lord Cornwallis in October 1781 ended the last major engagement of the American Revolution.

A. Map Exercises

1. Much happened in a small area on April 19, 1775. Using the map of the battles of Lexington and Concord, estimate the distance from Boston to Concord, and from Lexington to Concord.

2. On the map of the battles of Lexington and Concord, trace with a marker the British retreat from Concord to Meriam's Corner, where more fighting occurred, to Lexington, where still more fighting took place, to Arlington, then called Menotomy, where there was still more fighting, and so on, back to Boston.

3. The Revolutionary War map shows British troop movements, but not American. Draw in some of the major American movements:
    a. Benedict Arnold's advance on Quebec from Massachusetts through Maine in 1776.
    b. George Washington's activity in New Jersey and Pennsylvania in 1776–1777.
    c. Nathanael Greene's maneuvers in North Carolina in 1781.
    d. The positions of Washington and the Marquis de Lafayette in Virginia in 1781.

B. Further Exercises

1. According to the famous poem by Henry Wadsworth Longfellow, it was in the skirmish at Concord's North Bridge, "the rude bridge that arched the flood," where "the shot heard round the world" was fired. In what sense was it a "shot heard round the world"? And why did it occur at Concord, when fighting at Lexington earlier in the day had claimed several lives? Investigate these questions in a one- to two-page essay.

2. Obtain a contemporary map of Boston. Note that Boston Neck, the narrow strip of land connecting Boston with the mainland, is no longer present and that Charlestown and Roxbury are now part of the city. How do you explain these changes? What is the modern name of Winnisimmet?

3. The map of the Revolutionary War suggests that the war was organized so that armies in the field moved and wheeled and attacked with very specific objectives for each battle rather than following a broader scheme of defending and enlarging a block of territory. What evidence does the map provide for this strategy? Why was the war fought in this fashion?

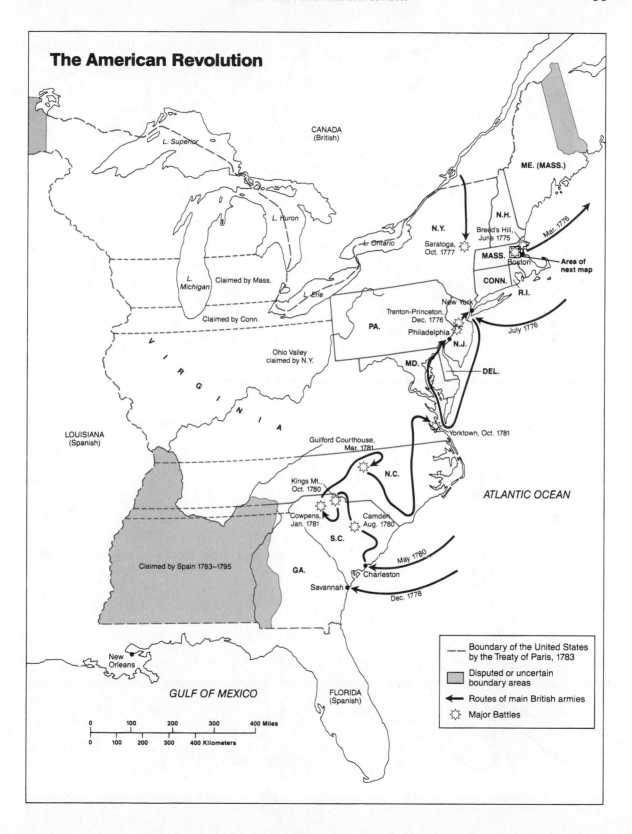

The American Revolution

CANADA
(British)

ME. (MASS.)

L. Superior

L. Huron

N.Y.

N.H.

Mar. 1776

L. Ontario

Saratoga,
Oct. 1777

Breed's Hill,
June 1775

MASS.
Boston

Area of
next map

L. Michigan

Claimed by Mass.

CONN.

R.I.

L. Erie

New York

July 1776

Claimed by Conn.

Trenton-Princeton,
Dec. 1776

PA.

Philadelphia

Ohio Valley
claimed by N.Y.

V
I
R
G
I
N
I
A

N.J.

MD.

DEL.

LOUISIANA
(Spanish)

Yorktown, Oct. 1781

Guilford Courthouse,
Mar. 1781

N.C.

ATLANTIC OCEAN

Kings Mt.,
Oct. 1780

Cowpens,
Jan. 1781

Camden,
Aug. 1780

Claimed by Spain 1783–1795

S.C.

May 1780

GA.

Charleston

Savannah

Dec. 1778

New
Orleans

GULF OF MEXICO

FLORIDA
(Spanish)

| 0 | 100 | 200 | 300 | 400 Miles |

| 0 | 100 | 200 | 300 | 400 Kilometers |

- - - Boundary of the United States
by the Treaty of Paris, 1783

Disputed or uncertain
boundary areas

← Routes of main British armies

☆ Major Battles

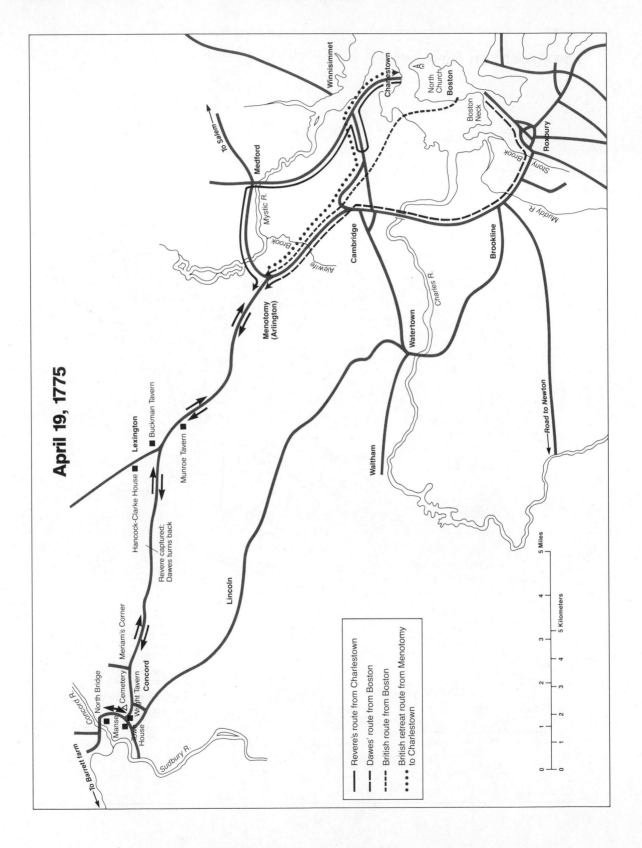

April 19, 1775

To Barrett farm
Concord R.
North Bridge
Manse
Cemetery
Meriam's Corner
Wright Tavern
Concord
Sudbury R.
Lincoln

Hancock-Clarke House
Lexington
Buckman Tavern
Munroe Tavern
Revere captured; Dawes turns back

Menotomy
(Arlington)

To Salem
Medford
Winnisimmet
Charlestown
Mystic R.
Alewife Brook
Cambridge
Watertown
Waltham
Charles R.
Brookline

North Church
Boston
Boston Neck
Roxbury
Stony Brook
Muddy R.
Road to Newton

Revere's route from Charlestown
Dawes' route from Boston
British route from Boston
British retreat route from Menotomy to Charlestown

5 Miles
5 Kilometers
0 1 2 3 4

Unit 5

Cession of Western Lands
After the American Revolution, 1783–1802

The existence of the United States as a single powerful entity was far from the minds of the political leaders of the 1780s. No such large republic had ever existed before, and the prospect of a national central government far from the control of its citizens threatened the very nature of republican government. The creation of small republics, on the other hand, would make them vulnerable to foreign power. The solution was federation, the joining together of small republics for a common purpose. That common purpose was the success of the Revolution, and the Second Continental Congress, which first met in May 1775, was soon serving as a national government. But the delegates to the Congress, believing a more permanent arrangement was necessary, by November 1777 agreed to present the Articles of Confederation to the legislatures of the thirteen states.

Debate over the Articles was sharp. Perhaps the single most serious dispute concerned who would control the lands to the West, beyond the Appalachian Mountains. Separation from Great Britain had dissolved the authority of the king, but it had not abrogated the colonial charters, which gave some states reason to claim lands in the West while other states remained "landless." The landless states wanted Congress to take control of the land beyond the mountains. It should be common property, they argued. The New Jersey delegation contended that the western lands had been procured "by the common blood and treasure of the whole." The landed states resisted the argument and instead gave themselves to disputing one another's overlapping claims.

But so pressing was the need to create a permanent union that all of the states except Maryland agreed to the Articles of Confederation. In refusing to accept the Articles, Maryland was also refusing to create the unanimity required to put the new government into effect. Underlying the Marylanders' resistance was the fear that the wealth of the landed states might permit those states to have such low taxes that the landless states would lose population to them. Perhaps a more important factor in Maryland's position was the crass self-interest of land speculators. Before the war, speculators from the landless states had been purchasing land from the Indians, often from individuals who lacked tribal authority for "selling" property. The speculators argued that Congress had inherited the king's authority over unoccupied lands, and they wanted Congress to recognize their claims. They would be defeated, they realized, by a guarantee in the Articles of Confederation that no state should be deprived of territory for the benefit of the United States. Maryland refused to agree.

Something had to be done to break the impasse if a permanent government was to be formed. In 1780 New York offered to cede—or yield—its western claims to Congress. Virginia then also agreed, but on condition that Congress not recognize any of the Indian purchases that speculators had made. The speculators saw their opportunity for profit vanishing, and many tried unsuccessfully to buy the influence of congressmen. Virginia's leaders attached another condition as well. Fearing that the size of the western territories was too great for successful republican government, they insisted that the lands be divided into several "republican states," to be admitted to the Union on equal terms with its original members.

After Virginia agreed to this transfer of claims, or cession, Maryland took steps to ratify the Articles. Slowly the other states as well followed Virginia's lead. The last of the thirteen was Georgia in 1802. The United States finally had a permanent central government as of March 1, 1781, less than eight months before the British surrender at Yorktown. There was much work yet to do before that central government could be made effective.

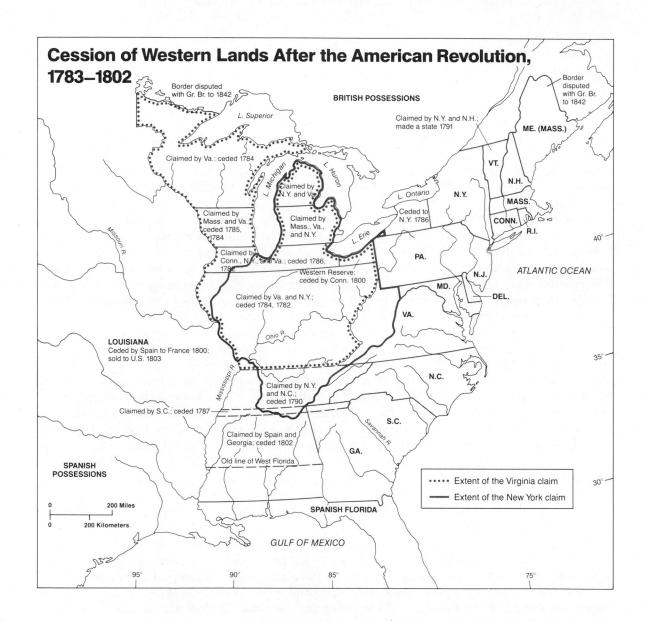

Cession of Western Lands After the American Revolution, 1783–1802

A. Map Exercises

1. Using the map as a guide, list the states that had western claims. List the six "landless" states as well.

2. Which state had the largest claim to western lands? List the names of contemporary states that have all or part of their lands lying within this claim.

3. All or part of which present-day states are to be found within lands ceded by Massachusetts? Connecticut? New York? Virginia? The Carolinas? Georgia?

B. Further Exercises

1. Colonial charters were granted at a time when the geography of North America was little known. Examine those charters to determine what wording permitted such extravagant western claims by some states, but not by others.

2. The wording of the charters also permitted some states to claim lands that other states vigorously argued belonged to them. Pick two such states for consideration, and in a one- to two-page paper, discuss which claims you believe to have been more valid.

3. Colonial charters were a sort of contract. Did the contracts dissolve when one of the contracting parties was fired from his job by the Declaration of Independence? Should they have?

Unit 6

The Old Northwest, 1785–1787

The United States attempted with varying results to deal with many severe problems in the years following the American Revolution. One of its most successful actions was the organization of the lands north of the Ohio River, a region thinly populated by squatters, Indians, and French and also by the British, who stubbornly held onto their military posts in order to maintain a lucrative fur trade with the Miami, Shawnee, Delaware, and Iroquois of the area and to lay the groundwork for future repossession.

In 1784 Congress established formal authority over this area, known as the Northwest. It was a time when the nation was in serious financial difficulty. Lacking authority to tax, Congress depended on the states to supply the national government with the funds necessary to function. When the states delayed or resisted, Congress began preparing to sell some of the newly acquired federal lands. The Ordinance of 1784 provided for territorial government and assured settlers that they would not remain in permanent colonial status. The Ordinance of 1785 provided that the Northwest be surveyed into townships six miles square along lines running east-west and north-south. These gridlike townships contained 36 sections of 640 acres each, and they give today's Midwest a markedly different appearance from the older settlements in the East. A section was the smallest unit that could be purchased. Townships and sections were to be sold for no less than a dollar an acre, to be paid in specie, or coin—that is, not in the devalued paper money that Congress had issued to finance the war.

While surveying was under way and before the lands were ready for public sale, speculators got into action. A group called the Ohio Company offered to buy a million and a half acres. The prospective purchasers would not, however, pay in specie. Despite its wish not to deal in depreciated currency, Congress was so pressed for funds that it accepted the offer. The Ohio Company also agreed to take an option on 5 million additional acres in the name of the Scioto Company—a group, it must be reported, that counted several congressmen among its members.

The Northwest Ordinance of 1787 further regulated the organization of the new territory. The ordinance stipulated that for each territory, there would be a period during which a governor, a secretary, and a court of three judges—all appointed by Congress—would hold full power. When the population reached 5,000 free adult males, a representative legislature would be established, which could send an observer to Congress. The governor, still appointed by Congress, was to have veto power over the actions of the legislature. The whole area was to be divided into not fewer than three nor more than five territories, and each would be admitted to the Union "on an equal footing with the original states in all respects whatsoever" when it attained a population of 60,000. Slaveowners already living in the region could retain their slaves, but the importation of any further slaves was prohibited. No person was to be "molested" for his religious beliefs. "Schools and the means of education" were to be encouraged, presumably by means of the Land Ordinance of 1785, which had already reserved one section in each township "for the maintenance of public schools."

Southern delegates in Congress accepted the restriction on slavery because they could look forward to slavery's expansion south of the Ohio River. The vast lands of the West seemed to hold opportunity for all. The organization of the Old Northwest set a worthy standard for the future.

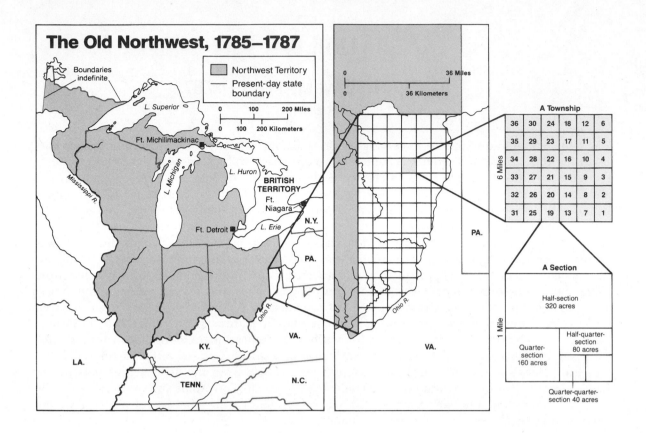

The Old Northwest, 1785–1787

A. Map Exercises

1. The Northwest Ordinance specified that not fewer than three nor more than five territories would be created north of the Ohio River and east of the Mississippi River. On the map, label the states that presently occupy the region.

2. Label the Northwest Territory's major rivers. Note carefully the position of the military posts as they were in 1787.

3. The Old Northwest is a region of immense importance to the United States today. Using information from the maps in Part II, pages 14, 16, 18, sketch in the region's physiographic characteristics, natural vegetation, and average rainfall and temperatures.

4. From the U.S. Agricultural Regions map on page 73, in Volume 2, sketch in information about the agricultural uses of the Old Northwest. From the Standard Metropolitan Statistical Areas map on pages 80–81, in Volume 2, list the region's major urban centers.

B. Further Exercises

1. The fact that the Northwest Ordinance provided for the admission of new states as equals with the old was of immense importance to the future of the nation. In a one- to two-page paper, speculate on what might have happened if Congress had decided to keep new territories permanently subordinate. Can you think of any arguments for doing so?

2. If you grew up on or near a farm, you probably have a fairly good conception of what constitutes an acre, a quarter-section, and a section. If you come from a city, you may have only a vague idea. Calculate how many square feet are in an acre. Calculate the length in linear feet along one side of an acre. How does that compare with, say, a certain number of football fields?

Unit 7

The West and the Mississippi River

In the early years of the American Republic, maintaining the cohesion of the nation was a serious problem. Vast distances separated the more settled areas on the East from the West. The British presence in what was the Old Northwest and the Spanish grip on what was then the Southwest posed serious dangers. The outposts of these European nations were beyond the effective reach of the American government. France and Spain formed alliances with the Indians and collaborated with unscrupulous Americans who sought personal advancement regardless of American national interests.

Overland travel was difficult, especially in the West. The flow of settlers accelerated only as adventurers cut new roads over the mountains. Still, one of the most efficient means of transportation was by river. For farmers in the West who wished to take goods to market, the downstream current was a boon.

Traveling on a mighty river can be dangerous, however. Eddies, sand bars, floating logs, and winter ice can delay or destroy a barge or a river boat. Thus travel generally must have been a daytime activity and, in the 1790s, arduous, dangerous, and time-consuming. But what alternative did the voyager have? What good fortune it was for the United States to have a river system like that of the Mississippi and its tributaries.

Unfortunately for the United States, this important Mississippi River route was vulnerable to foreign pressure. Since the destruction of the French North American empire during the Seven Years' War, Spain had controlled all of the west bank of the river and both banks for the last 200 miles. Spain also laid claim to the Mississippi Territory of the United States and to the western portions of Tennessee and Kentucky.

In 1795 John Jay, who had been Secretary of Foreign Affairs during the Confederation period and was an experienced diplomat, concluded a treaty with Great Britain that defused a potentially explosive situation. The U.S. government had sent Jay to seek settlement of a number of problems between the two nations. Jay was partially successful, but the treaty was enormously unpopular in the United States because it did not deal with the issue of the British practice of seizing American seamen and impressing them into British service. It did, however, provide for an easing of tensions between the two nations—a development carefully noted in the court of Spain.

Thomas Pinckney was chosen to try to resolve American problems with Spain, and he arrived in Madrid in 1795 seeking a treaty. Spain was willing to sell the right to navigate the Mississippi for a consideration: that the Americans would guarantee the Spanish territorial possessions on its banks. After some months of impasse, Pinckney threatened to return home but agreement was eventually reached, for Spain feared losing the goodwill of the United States. The treaty assured both parties full rights to navigation of the Mississippi from source to mouth. The northern boundary of Florida was settled at the 31st parallel. Spain agreed to designate the port of New Orleans as a place of deposit. Goods could be stored for up to three years without payment of duty while they awaited an opportunity for transshipment. After three years the arrangement could be renewed.

The Treaty of San Lorenzo concluded by Thomas Pinckney was ratified by the U.S. Senate in 1796. At least temporarily, it brought a degree of stability to the region. Louisiana was soon returned by Spain to the French and later, in 1803, was purchased by the United States. East of the river, Spanish Florida remained a bone of contention. Border crossings and armed conflict continued, despite the treaty.

A. Map Exercises

1. On the map, notice the general directions in which the rivers flow. What topographical feature explains this pattern in, say, Pennsylvania or Virginia? On the map, write in these important locations: Pittsburgh, New Orleans, the Appalachian Mountains. Is Pittsburgh a western city? Was it in 1795?

2. If a farmer in southern Ohio wished to travel to New Orleans, how might he have done it? Mark the Ohio, the Wabash, the Mississippi, and the Yazoo rivers on the map. If the rivers flow at three to six miles per hour, how long would the trip take?

3. How might U.S. history and the U.S. economy have been different if the rivers flowed north into icy wastes—as do the five major rivers of Siberia? How might they have been different if the mouth of the Mississippi had remained forever outside the jurisdiction of the United States?

4. On the map, lightly shade in the area of the entire Spanish claim east of the Mississippi. Mark the northern boundary of Florida at 31°. How far is New Orleans from the actual mouth of the Mississippi River? Consider the uncertainty of navigational schedules both for river transport and for vessels plying the open seas of the Gulf of Mexico. Why was the right of deposit without payment of duty so important?

B. Further Exercises

1. Just south of the 31st parallel in West Florida is a major coastal feature. What is the name of the bay?

2. Is there any difference between the designation 31° and reference to the 31st parallel?

3. The Tennessee River did not provide the same navigational advantages as did the Ohio. Why not?

4. Write in the names of five unlabeled rivers that also served as valuable commercial routes in the late eighteenth century.

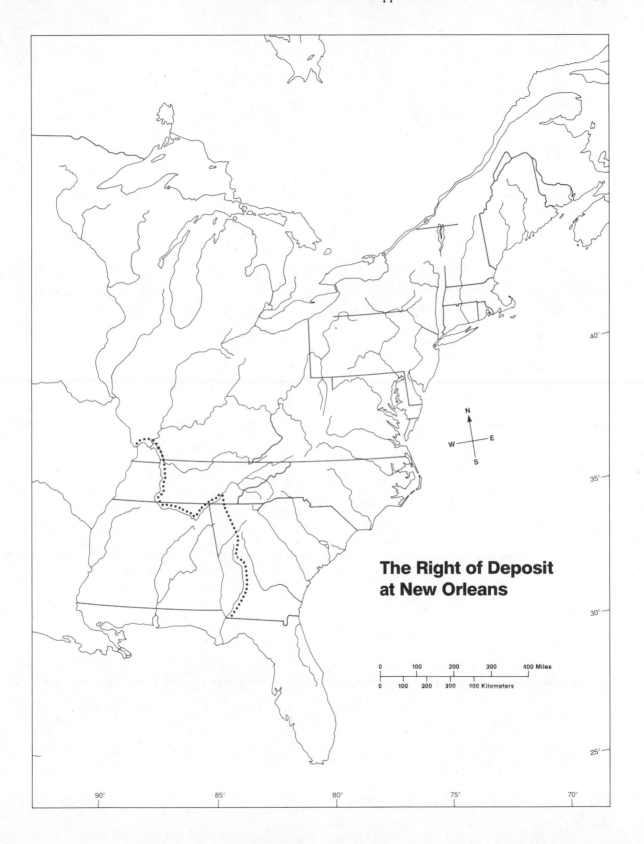

The Right of Deposit at New Orleans

Unit 8

The Louisiana Purchase and Exploration

Beyond the Mississippi River lay an immense territory that belonged to Spain at the end of the eighteenth century. In 1800 Napoleon Bonaparte negotiated a secret treaty to transfer to France the portion known as Louisiana. President Thomas Jefferson learned of the agreement in 1801, before France formally took possession of the region. Jefferson and other Americans were disturbed. When the Spanish governor at New Orleans suspended the right of deposit in that city in 1802, Jefferson viewed the action as an unhappy omen of future French policy toward the United States. A considerable portion of America's produce passed through New Orleans on its way to market. When that city came under French control, the United States would have to reopen an alliance with Great Britain to protect itself and the commerce of the West.

Jefferson was disposed to attempt negotiation before action. He instructed Robert R. Livingston, the American minister in Paris, to try to purchase New Orleans and the Floridas. The president also obtained an appropriation from Congress of $2 million and sent James Monroe as a special envoy to assist Livingston. Jefferson privately authorized Monroe to bid as high as $10 million if necessary. When Monroe arrived, he was astonished to discover that French foreign minister Talleyrand was offering to sell the whole of Louisiana to the United States. Livingston and Monroe hesitated only briefly before agreeing to the Louisiana Purchase.

There were a number of reasons why France had determined to sell Louisiana. First, French troops had failed to defeat a revolution in Saint Domingue, now Haiti. This loss cost France an important military base in the Caribbean, necessary for an effective occupation of Louisiana. In addition, a renewal of war between France and Great Britain seemed certain. Napoleon wished to have his troops in Europe, and he also wanted the money that the sale of Louisiana would bring. Furthermore, Napoleon anticipated future American ambitions in Louisiana. Resumption of friendly relations between Britain and the United States would put the British fleet between France and Louisiana.

Although westerners were well satisfied with the purchase, New England Federalists reacted with alarm. They were dismayed by so great an increase in the public debt to buy nothing but unknown empty land, and they feared that the new states that would ultimately come from Louisiana would weaken the importance of the older East and strengthen Jefferson's Republican party. Federalist extremists even talked of forming a northern confederacy and seceding from the Union.

The price tag for Louisiana's 828,000 square miles—an area that *doubled* the size of the United States—was $15 million. The boundaries of the territory were defined merely as being the same as during Spanish possession; a more precise definition remained for the future. President Jefferson at first had worried deeply that he might be exceeding the constitutional limits of his power in making the purchase. In the beginning of the negotiations, he had wanted an amendment to the Constitution to permit acquiring territory from which new states might be created. Ultimately concerned, however, that delay would mean loss of the opportunity, Jefferson in time swallowed his doubts and submitted the treaty to the Senate for ratification.

In January 1803, even before Monroe had gone to France and the United States obtained Louisiana, Congress had secretly appropriated money for an expedition to explore the upper reaches of the Missouri River and the remote Oregon Country. Jefferson had been trying to promote such an expedition for years. His interest was scientific, but he also was aware that exploration of unknown territory confers advantage on later claimants. The two leaders of the expedition—Meriwether Lewis, Jefferson's private secretary, and William Clark, a captain in the United States Army—were instructed to study the flora and fauna and keep an eye out for mineral deposits and trading opportunities. Lewis had earlier been sent to Philadelphia to learn methods of taking latitude and longitude and the use of astronomical instruments. The Lewis and Clark expedition left in the spring of 1804. Their route followed the Missouri River from mouth to source and beyond. After initial difficulty with some bands of Sioux, the expedition wintered with the Mandan Indians in what is now the state of North Dakota. They were joined by a French-Canadian fur trader and his wife, a Shoshone named Sacajawea, guides for the journey. The party of forty-five continued up the Missouri, through the Rocky Mountains via the Bitterroot Valley and Lolo Pass to the Columbia River. There they constructed canoes that took them to the Pacific. They built Fort Clatsop not far from present-day Astoria for the winter of 1805–1806 and then returned, reaching St. Louis in September 1806. They brought back a large botanical collection, maps, sketches and journals, and information of value to the fur trade, and they had strengthened the foundation for an American claim to Oregon.

The government authorized other expeditions in Louisiana as well, including two journeys undertaken by Zebulon Pike. On the first, in 1805, up the Mississippi River in search of its source, Pike got as far as Leech Lake in northern Minnesota. Thinking that he had found what he was seeking, he turned back. In 1806 he was commissioned to go west to the Spanish borderlands. Departing from St. Louis, he crossed the Ozark Plateau to the Arkansas River. He found Pike's Peak, which he designated "unclimbable." Pike eventually reached the Rio Grande, where the Spanish authorities intercepted his party. Pike characterized the Southwest as desertlike and inhospitable, a description that endured for years to come.

When first joined to the United States, Louisiana was a vast unknown territory. Luck and the ability to react quickly made its acquisition possible. Within a short time its value became evident. Thoughtful political leaders and intrepid explorers had opened the way.

A. Map Exercises

1. The addition of the Louisiana Territory doubled the size of the United States. On the map, sketch in and label the present-day states that occupy its territory.

2. The Bitterroot River Valley through which the Lewis and Clark expedition passed lies on Idaho's eastern boundary. Mark it. Note the point at which the rivers in the West all flow in the general direction of the Pacific.

3. Astoria and Fort Clatsop lie near the mouth of the Columbia River. Locate them on the map and mark the locations.

4. The importance of the acquisition of Louisiana was evident even to Talleyrand. Using information from the maps in Part II, sketch in the physiographic characteristics, natural vegetation, and average rainfall and temperatures of the territory.

5. From the U.S. Agricultural Regions map on page 73 in Volume 2, sketch in information about the current agricultural uses of the land that made up the Louisiana Territory.

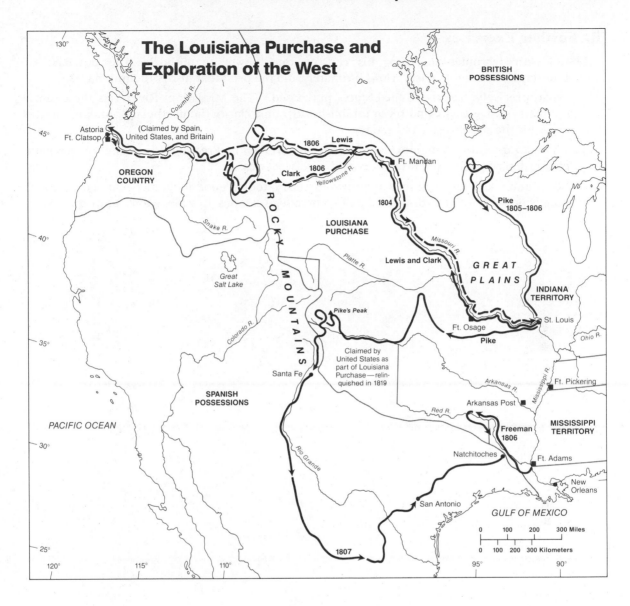

The Louisiana Purchase and Exploration of the West

BRITISH POSSESSIONS

130°

45°

Astoria
Ft. Clatsop
(Claimed by Spain, United States, and Britain)

Columbia R.

OREGON COUNTRY

1806 Lewis

Clark 1806

Yellowstone R.

Ft. Mandan

Pike 1805–1806

Snake R.

40°

LOUISIANA PURCHASE

1804

Lewis and Clark

Missouri R.

GREAT PLAINS

Great Salt Lake

Platte R.

INDIANA TERRITORY

Pike's Peak

Ft. Osage

St. Louis

35°

Colorado R.

Claimed by United States as part of Louisiana Purchase—relinquished in 1819

Pike

Ohio R.

Santa Fe

SPANISH POSSESSIONS

Arkansas R.

Ft. Pickering

Red R.

Arkansas Post

Freeman 1806

MISSISSIPPI TERRITORY

PACIFIC OCEAN

30°

Rio Grande

Natchitoches

Ft. Adams

New Orleans

San Antonio

GULF OF MEXICO

25°

1807

0   100   200   300 Miles

0 100 200 300 Kilometers

120°   115°   110°   95°   90°

R O C K Y   M O U N T A I N S

B. Further Exercises

1. Jefferson's scruples regarding his constitutional power to authorize the purchase of Louisiana were sorely tried. How, ultimately, did the president justify the purchase?

2. What, precisely, had the United States purchased? The Mississippi River was the eastern boundary. Investigate and try to establish with some clarity the northern boundary; do the same for the southwestern boundary.

3. The map indicates that an exploration was undertaken by Freeman. In a one- to two-page paper, describe the man, his travels, and his discoveries.

4. Lewis and Clark traveled into unknown territory, took a good look, and mapped it. Mapping is not easy. Try to draw a map of your college campus, to scale, without any guides.

Unit 9

Territorial Growth of the United States to 1853

At the beginning of the seventeenth century, America was just a beachhead. By the end of the eighteenth century, an independent nation, it stretched from the Atlantic coast to the Mississippi River, and from the Great Lakes to the Floridas. Within a few more years, the nation doubled in size, as we have seen, with the addition of Louisiana.

Further boundary adjustments did not come until the years following the War of 1812. In 1815 a commercial treaty between the United States and Great Britain removed many restrictions on Anglo-American trade. When James Monroe assumed the presidency in 1817, he chose as his secretary of state the brilliant John Quincy Adams. In that same year the Rush-Bagot Treaty was made with Great Britain. It effectively demilitarized the Great Lakes by restricting the number of ships that the two powers could maintain there. The agreement further provided that either side could terminate it on six months' notice, but the policy became permanent and eventually led to the absence of armament along the entire American-Canadian border. The British-American Convention of 1818 fixed the demilitarized boundary from the Lake of the Woods to the Rocky Mountains at 49° north latitude. The agreement also provided for the resumption of American fishing rights off Newfoundland and for joint occupation of the Oregon Country for the next ten years. Happily for the future, it was this series of settlements rather than the War of 1812 that was the portent of ongoing relations between the two nations. In 1842 the Senate ratified the Webster-Ashburton Treaty, finally resolving the difficult problems of the Canadian-American boundary between Lake Superior and the Lake of the Woods, as well as fixing the northern limits of the state of Maine.

After Louisiana joined the United States, the Americans made the best case they could for its broadest possible extent. The boundaries were ill defined, and the bordering Spanish lands in West Florida and parts of New Spain were in dispute. In West Florida in 1810 and 1812, the United States simply took over, adding a part to Louisiana and another part to the Mississippi Territory. Spain had an equally tenuous hold on East Florida. In 1818 Andrew Jackson, the American military commander in the South, led an invading force into Florida. Spain was responsible for control of Florida's Seminole Indians, who had been launching raids into the United States. Jackson retaliated by seizing Pensacola and another fort, deposing the Spanish governor, hanging two British subjects, and raising the American flag. Spain, Secretary of State Adams asserted, should govern Florida effectively or cede it to the United States. In 1819 Spain agreed to the Adams-Onís Treaty, also known as the Transcontinental Treaty. It secured the Floridas for the United States and established a boundary with New Spain that ran from the Mississippi River along the Sabine River and then west along the Red and Arkansas rivers to the Rocky Mountains. From there it followed the 49th parallel to the Pacific Ocean.

Later, in 1844, James K. Polk based much of his campaign for the presidency on the growing spirit of Manifest Destiny—specifically, on the United States' acquisition of Texas and Oregon. The circumstances surrounding the addition of Texas to the United States are noted in this book in relation to the map of the Texas Revolution of 1836 and the Mexican War, 1846–1848, on page 79.

At about the same time, settlement of the question of Oregon was reached. In April 1846 Polk secured from Congress termination of the joint British-American occupation of Oregon, which had been renewed periodically since first negotiated. One year's notice was required for termination, and this the British received. British claims extended south and east from the coast to the Columbia River. American claims in Oregon reached to 54° 40′ north latitude, the southern-most boundary of Russian Alaska. Polk knew that he could not obtain such an expanse of territory without going to war, but he wished to avoid war, particularly because trouble with Mexico loomed. In the case of Great Britain, unwillingness to fight was influenced by the numbers of American settlers who had been entering Oregon and by a declining fur trade. In the end both sides agreed to negotiate. The resulting Buchanan-Pakenham Treaty extended the British-American boundary of 49° to Puget Sound. Britain kept all of Vancouver Island and retained navigation rights on the Columbia River. The Senate ratified the treaty in 1846, with the proviso that British navigation rights on the Columbia were temporary.

War with Mexico resulted in the addition of millions of square miles to the United States in circumstances described in connection with the map of the Mexican War. In 1853 the Gadsden Purchase was made. It is mentioned in discussion of the map of the Kansas-Nebraska Act of 1854, page 85.

All of the land that makes up the contiguous 48 states was thus acquired by 1853. In 1867 the United States purchased Alaska from Russia and in 1898 acquired Hawaii as a result of imperialist adventures overseas. These are presently the 50 states of the Union.

A. Map Exercises

1. The great size of the United States affords the nation a variety of climatic conditions. Draw a line through the Middle Atlantic states at the same latitude as the northern boundary of California. Compare the two areas in regard to average rainfall and temperature by using the map in Part II (page 18).

2. In like fashion, compare Texas west of 100° west longitude near, say, Midland, and the Sea Islands of Georgia. How do you account for the differences?

3. More than simply taking advantage of a weakened Spain, the United States' acquisition of West Florida in 1810 and 1812 added a valuable seaport. Name it and the rivers that serve it.

4. The boundary lines determined by the Transcontinental Treaty presently form parts of the boundaries of a number of states. Mark those boundaries and name the states.

B. Further Exercises

1. The latitude of the city of Quebec is also the latitude of parts of Maine and of Vancouver Island. Compare their climatological conditions.

2. Some of the territory east of the Lake of the Woods, assured to the United States by the Webster-Ashburton Treaty, has unusually great value. Explain why.

3. Prior to the Webster-Ashburton Treaty, local people in northern Maine and New Brunswick actually attacked one another in their land dispute. What is the economic character of the region today?

4. Some people are always willing to fight. The United States did go to war with Mexico for the Southwest. The compromise settlements in Maine and Oregon, on the other hand, left some people disgruntled. Was it right to compromise instead of fight? Investigate this question in a one- to two-page paper.

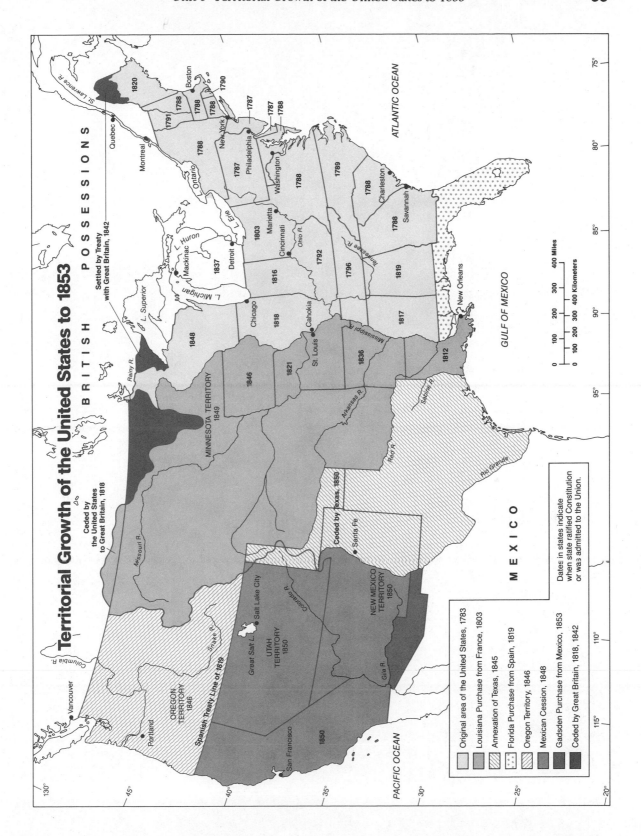

Territorial Growth of the United States to 1853

BRITISH POSSESSIONS

Settled by Treaty
with Great Britain, 1842

Ceded by
the United States
to Great Britain, 1818

ATLANTIC OCEAN

1820

Boston
1788
1791   1788 1790
1788   1787
New York   1787   1788
1788
Philadelphia   1787
Washington   1788   1789
1788
Quebec
Montreal
Ontario
L. Huron
L. Erie
1803
Marietta   Charleston   1788
Cincinnati   1788
Detroit   Ohio R.   Savannah
Mackinac   1837   1816   1792   1796   1819
L. Michigan
L. Superior   Chicago   1818   Cahokia   1817
Rainy R.   St. Louis   1836   1812
1848   New Orleans
GULF OF MEXICO

St. Lawrence R.

MINNESOTA TERRITORY
1849
1846   1821
Missouri R.
Arkansas R.
Red R.
Sabine R.
Rio Grande

MEXICO

Ced by Texas, 1850

Santa Fe
NEW MEXICO
TERRITORY
1850

Salt Lake City
Great Salt L.
Colorado R.
UTAH
TERRITORY
1850
Gila R.
1850

Snake R.
Columbia R.
Vancouver
Portland
OREGON
TERRITORY
1846
Spanish Treaty Line of 1819

San Francisco

PACIFIC OCEAN

Dates in states indicate
when state ratified Constitution
or was admitted to the Union.

	Original area of the United States, 1783
	Louisiana Purchase from France, 1803
	Annexation of Texas, 1845
	Florida Purchase from Spain, 1819
	Oregon Territory, 1846
	Mexican Cession, 1848
	Gadsden Purchase from Mexico, 1853
	Ceded by Great Britain, 1818, 1842

400 Miles
0   100   200   300   400 Kilometers

130°   45°   40°   35°   30°   25°   20°
75°   80°   85°   90°   95°   110°   115°

Unit 10

The Removal of Native Americans to the West, 1820 – 1840

At the beginning of the nineteenth century, some 60,000 Choctaw, Chickasaw, Cherokee, Creek, and Seminole Indians held millions of acres in southeastern United States. The Cherokee Indians, in the preceding decades, had made a transformation from communal ownership to private property, and many had moved into traditional towns, complete with mills and stores. Some had adapted so well to white ways that they became slaveowners. But the Cherokee were under extreme pressure to give up their lands in Tennessee, Georgia, and the western Carolinas to white settlement. The other members of the so-called Five Civilized Tribes of the Southeast also suffered as a result of the land hunger of whites. Native Americans lost millions of acres through encroachment and legal chicanery. In 1827 the Cherokee drew up a written constitution and declared themselves an independent nation holding full sovereignty over their lands. In 1829 the Cherokee government prescribed the death penalty for any tribal member who transferred land to white ownership without authority.

President Andrew Jackson in 1829 recommended removal of the southeastern tribes from the region. In that same year contention arose between the Cherokee nation and the state of Georgia. The Georgia legislature responded to the Cherokee constitution by declaring illegal the legislature created for Cherokee self-government and asserting that the Cherokee fell under the state's jurisdiction. Then in 1830, the U.S. Congress passed an Indian Removal Act that authorized the president to set up districts west of the Mississippi River for transfer of the Indians. Meanwhile, the discovery of gold on Cherokee land brought a rush of prospective miners within the native Americans' boundaries. The Cherokee nation sued to keep whites out of its territory. In 1831 the Supreme Court denied Georgia's right to extend state laws over the Cherokee people, but another ruling held that the Cherokee could not under the U.S. Constitution bring suit in federal courts. The Court did say, however, that the Cherokee were entitled to federal protection against intruders in their lands.

President Jackson ignored the Supreme Court. He set about encouraging Indian tribes to sell their tribal lands in exchange for new lands in Oklahoma and Arkansas. Jackson sent the Choctaw people a blunt message: if they refused to move, he would destroy them. In 1831 the Choctaw nation became the first to be uprooted and moved to the West, along a route later known as the Trail of Tears. Many migrants died from malnutrition, exposure, and cholera. In 1836 the Creek also suffered the hardships of removal. Those who resisted were sent on their trek in chains. About 3,500 members of the tribe's population of 15,000 died on the way.

By 1835, harassment, intimidation, and bribery had persuaded a minority of Cherokee chiefs to agree to removal, but most still resisted. In 1837 and 1838 the United States Army evicted the Cherokee from their land, gathered them in stockades, and sent them on the Trail of Tears to Oklahoma. Perhaps a quarter of the 15,000 who set out met death along the way. The Chickasaw suffered a similar fate. The Seminole fought to try to avoid deportation. During the struggle, the federal government forcibly removed most of the Seminole from the Florida territory. In 1842 it gave up the effort and permitted a small group of resisters to remain. The Sac and Fox of the Iowa-Illinois region were also overcome and sent west.

Indian removal opened the East to enormous economic expansion and the development of what later became the Cotton Kingdom of Georgia, Alabama, and Mississippi. As for the Indians, although President Jackson and the Removal Act of 1830 both promised to protect and forever guarantee their new lands in the West, they soon found those lands no more secure than they had been in the East.

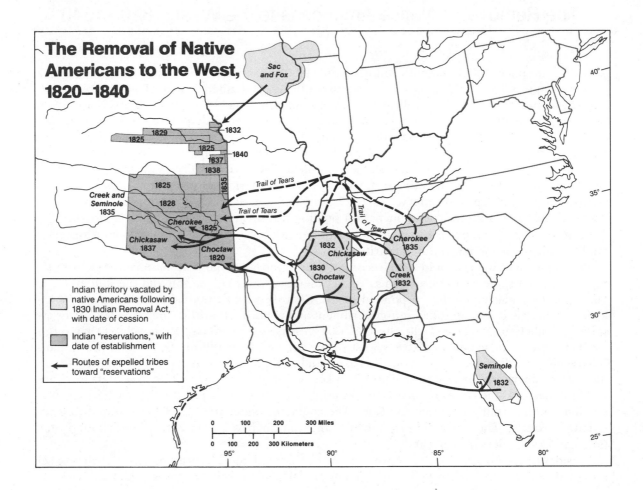

The Removal of Native Americans to the West, 1820–1840

A. Map Exercises

1. On the map, follow the trail of each of the Five Civilized Tribes, as well as that of the Sac and Fox, from their homeland to the new land they were forced to occupy in the West. For each, list the states and territories through which they passed, and estimate the distance traveled.

2. Again following the migrants' journeys, list the rivers used or crossed by each of the tribes on its route.

3. The areas from which the southeastern tribes were deported became highly significant in the regional and national economies. Using maps located elsewhere in this book, draw and label on this map the center of cotton culture in 1860 and the major cities and towns of the present day. Sketch in the major highways of the interstate highway system. Refer to the map on page 63 in Volume 1 and the maps on pages 65 and 80–81 in Volume 2.)

B. Further Exercises

1. Note from the map that several tribes occupied distinct areas in the Indian Territory in the West. How long did they remain secure in these areas? On the map, mark the changes that took place.

2. The death rate on the Trail of Tears was astonishingly high for people accustomed to outdoor life. Why was this so?

3. Why were the Five Civilized Tribes called by that name? If they were civilized, how could the Congress and the president of the United States feel justified in taking their land?

4. If Indians could have voted for the members of the Georgia legislature in 1829, how might Cherokee history have turned out differently? Would the map show a compromise in regard to landholding? Speculate on the answers to these questions in a one- to two-page paper.

Unit 11

King Cotton and Slavery

Even late in the eighteenth century, cotton cultivation in the South was largely confined to the Sea Islands of Georgia and South Carolina, where the soil and climate were excellent for long-staple cotton. The hardier short-staple cotton could have been cultivated successfully across large areas of the South, but it was exceedingly difficult to clean. Its sticky seeds resisted extraction from the plant's fibers. Then in 1793 Eli Whitney invented the cotton gin, a machine that, even before any refinement in its operation, sped up by fifty times the rate at which cotton could be cleaned.

At the same time that the preparation of cotton for market was made easier, demand for the fiber was increasing. In England, new textile factories with spinning and weaving machines needed greater and greater quantities of raw cotton. In 1800 the South produced 73,145 bales of cotton, but by 1820 the number had reached 334,378, and cotton accounted for more than half of United States agricultural exports.

With the advent of the cotton gin, new lands were brought into cultivation and large-scale farming of cotton increased in value and importance. The planting, cultivation, harvesting, ginning, and loading of cotton on the docks had traditionally fallen to slaves, and so hand in hand with the spread of cotton culture came a tremendous increase in the need for slave labor. Slavery consequently became a more deeply entrenched part of southern life.

Although more acres were devoted to corn than to cotton, the fluffy white staple was the largest cash crop of all; cotton was "king." The mainstay of the southern economy, cotton benefited the North and West as well. Northern merchants and bankers profited by shipping, insuring, and marketing the crop. Northern manufacturers transformed it into thread and cloth in their humming mills and factories. Western farmers found a major market for their food production in the cotton-growing South.

By 1840 the South was producing 1.35 million bales of cotton. Output reached 2.85 million bales in 1849 and peaked at 4.8 million bales in 1860. As new lands were opened, cotton production and population moved west. By the 1830s the center of cotton production had shifted from South Carolina and Georgia to Alabama and Mississippi. By the 1850s cotton growing had reached Arkansas, Louisiana, and eastern Texas. Conditions in the older states also contributed to population shifts. Beginning in the 1820s, soil depletion affected the states of the Upper South, and they underwent a long depression that lowered tobacco and cotton prices. Many Upper South growers shifted to grain production, which required less labor. As a result, a profitable slave trade developed between Virginia and the states of the "newer" South.

Although Congress formally had ended the external slave trade in 1808, enforcement of the ban was weak. Africans continued to be smuggled into North America until the end of the Civil War. The great increase in slaves did not, however, mainly stem from this illegal trade, but rather from natural reproduction—the excess of African Americans' births over deaths. The 1.5 million slaves in 1820 increased to 4 million in 1860, paralleling the growth in the southern economy.

Some 75 percent of southern whites owned no slaves. Most were self-sufficient farmers. But the region was dominated by the production of cotton and by a labor system and a social system that rested on the institution of slavery. The availability of new land, a self-reproducing supply of cheap labor, and low-cost river transportation down the Mississippi and other rivers helped keep cotton "king."

A. Map Exercises

1. The Mississippi River became a major route for the transportation of cotton and other products. River transportation was important throughout the South. Label all the southern rivers that appear on the map.

2. Using the maps as a guide, list those states that increased the area devoted to cotton production between 1820 and 1860. Which state seems to have had the greatest growth in the acreage given to the production of cotton?

3. Using the maps as a guide, list the states that showed an increase in slave population between 1820 and 1860. Which individual state seems to have had the greatest rise in the number of slaves?

B. Further Exercises

1. The topography of the South is described in broad terms as coastal plain, piedmont, and mountain. Using the Physiographic Map of the United States on page 14 in Part II and other sources, estimate what proportion of southern cotton was grown in each of the three regions in 1820; in 1860.

2. Not all southern blacks were slaves. Research the matter, and find out how many were free. What kind of work did free blacks do? Where did they live? Write a one- to two-page paper on these questions. Indicate major centers of the free-black population on the map.

3. Sea Island cotton is still highly valued. Investigate the reasons why. Ascertain what characteristics of Sea Island cotton explain its appeal.

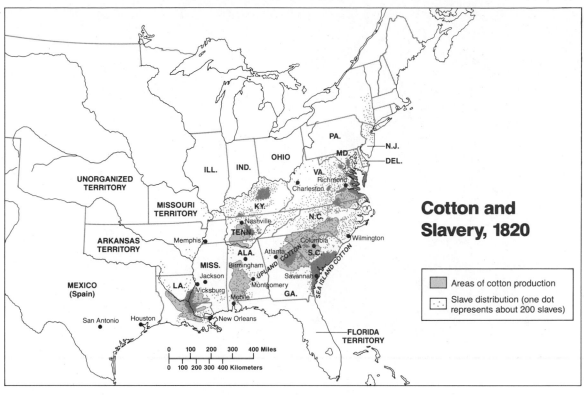

Cotton and Slavery, 1820

Areas of cotton production

Slave distribution (one dot represents about 200 slaves)

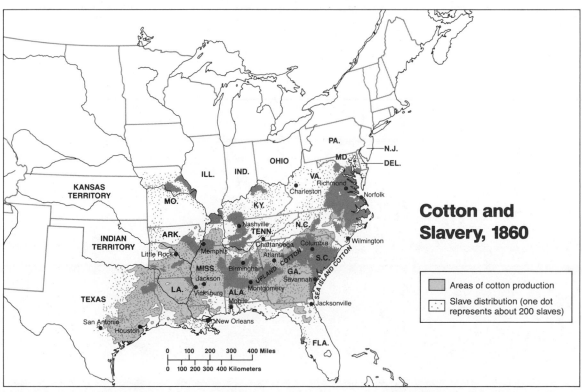

Cotton and Slavery, 1860

Areas of cotton production

Slave distribution (one dot represents about 200 slaves)

Unit 12

Main Roads, Canals, and River and Lake Transportation Before 1860
Railroads, 1850 – 1861

The success of American economic development has depended on a number of factors, not least among them a hospitable geographic environment and the development of transportation networks that connect the many parts of an integrated economic structure. At the beginning of the nineteenth century, the lack of reliable low-cost transportation greatly impeded economic development. The first important advance was the building of either graded and planked or macadamized* turnpikes or toll roads by private corporations. By the 1820s the Baltimore Turnpike extended to Cumberland, Maryland, and the National Road to Wheeling and then to Vandalia, Illinois. The Lancaster Turnpike and the Forbes Road went to Pittsburgh, and the Mohawk and Genesee Turnpike ran through New York to Lake Erie.

Turnpikes somewhat reduced the cost of transporting freight, but because water transportation was still cheaper, farmers often shipped their produce downstream. Steam power was the solution to improving upstream travel, and the first successful steamboat made the trip up the Hudson River from New York City to Albany in 1807. Steamboats were fast and cheap, carrying freight upriver for about one-tenth the cost of using keelboats poled along by hand.

The construction of canals connecting major waterways further improved water transportation. In 1825 New York State opened the Erie Canal, spanning the 350 miles between Albany and Buffalo on Lake Erie. Within a short time the cost of transporting a ton of freight between New York City and Buffalo fell from nearly twenty cents to under two cents, and the time required dropped from twenty days to six. Philadelphia and Baltimore also developed canal systems of their own. Illinois, Indiana, and Ohio constructed canals that connected the Ohio and Mississippi rivers with the Great Lakes. By 1840 there were 3,326 miles of canals, and the nation had a complete internal waterway from New York City to New Orleans.

Government played a major role in financing transportation developments. State and local governments often supported turnpike companies by granting them land or subscribing to their stock; it was the states that built most of the important canals. Federal and state governments also paid for river and harbor improvements. During these years the federal role remained smaller than that of the states and localities.

Speed and cost were major considerations in transportation. In 1828 construction began on the Baltimore and Ohio Railroad. Baltimore merchants hoped to compete with New York for the growing trade of the interior. By 1840 there were 3,000 miles of track, most of it in the Northeast, and another 5,000 miles were laid during the next decade. In the 1850s railroad mileage expanded dramatically, with some part of it given to consolidating small independent lines into larger trunk lines. In the South, however, most railroad lines continued to be short and to serve merely as feeders to river transportation. By 1860 the railroad system was primarily one that united the Northwest with the Northeast. In the Northwest various lines in Ohio,

---

Macadamized: paved with layers of compacted stones that are bound together with a material such as tar.

Indiana, and Illinois connected the Ohio and Mississippi rivers with the Great Lakes. Others ran eastward from Chicago to link with eastern trunk lines. The arrangement made Chicago the bustling center of western railroad activity.

Most funds for eastern railroad construction came from American and British investors, with help from state and local government subsidies. In the West public support was more important and state and local governments aided the railroads with loans, subsidies, and stock subscriptions. In 1850 Congress passed the first of many railroad land-grant laws, giving the Illinois Central Railroad three square miles of land in alternate sections on both sides of a proposed line; that is, six square miles for each mile of track. Southern support for the measure was obtained by making a similar grant for a line from the Ohio River to Mobile, Alabama. By 1860 approximately 28 million acres from the public domain had been granted to the states or directly to the railroads for railroad construction.

Development of a transcontinental railroad became a matter of controversy during the 1850s as sectional rivalry prevented agreement on route and location. Before anything could be done, the Civil War halted plans altogether. After that great conflict, however, the nation saw a renewed boom in railroad building.

A. Map Exercises

1. On the Main Roads map, trace the routes of the turnpikes described in the first paragraph of this unit.

2. Using the Main Roads map, trace a water route from New York City to Cincinnati. List the cities and states served by the route you chose. Can you identify more than one route?

3. Continue by water from Cincinnati to Natchez, Mississippi. List the cities and states the route touches. Do the same for the water route from Cincinnati to Galena, Illinois.

4. Using the Railroads map, trace a route by rail from Philadelphia to Detroit. List the cities and states touched by the route. Estimate the proportion of the trip dependent on construction completed after 1850.

5. According to the map, which cities in the South were best served by railroads before the Civil War?

B. Further Exercises

1. Note the relative absence of major roads, canals, and railroads in parts of Pennsylvania, Virginia, and Kentucky. What geographical explanation can you suggest?

2. The map shows relatively little emphasis on canal building in the South. What hypothesis can you offer in explanation?

3. One of the important attributes of a transportation network is dependability. Many of the nation's major canals were inoperable during part of the year. Why? What effect might this circumstance have had on railroad growth?

4. In a one- to two-page paper, describe the railroad that serves your college or university or the town nearest to it. Also discuss when was it built, whether government funds or government lands were involved, and what other cities this rail line serves.

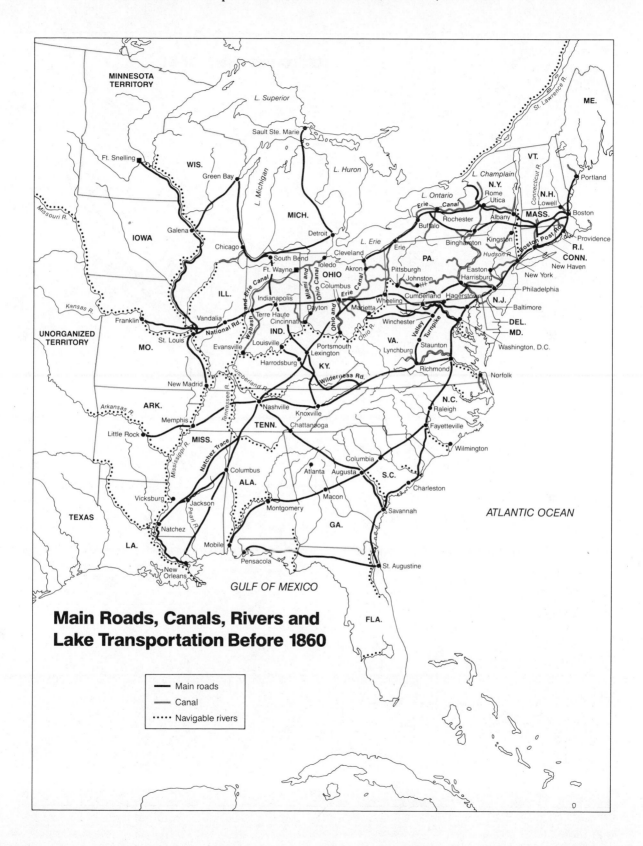

Main Roads, Canals, Rivers and Lake Transportation Before 1860

— Main roads
— Canal
···· Navigable rivers

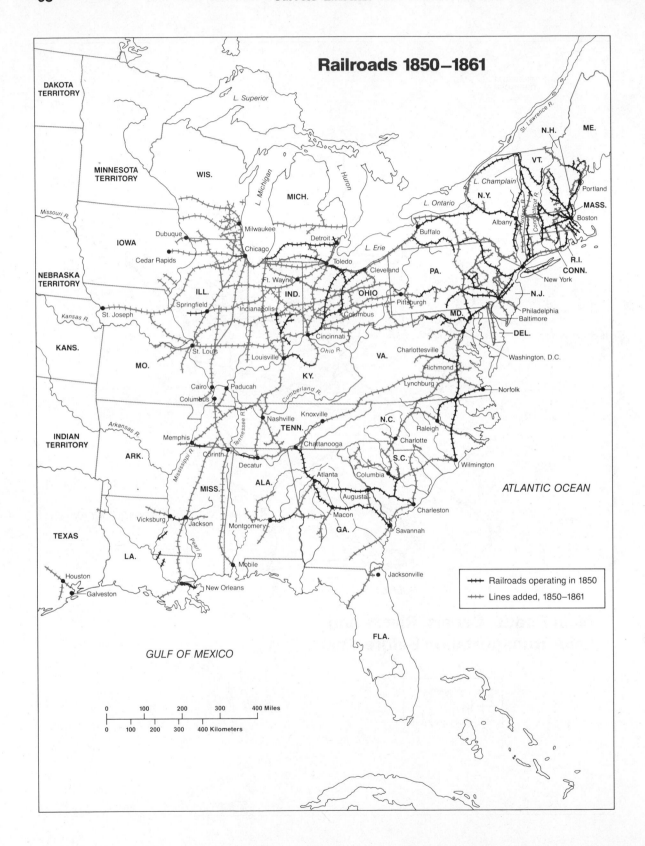

Railroads 1850–1861

DAKOTA
TERRITORY

MINNESOTA
TERRITORY

NEBRASKA
TERRITORY

KANS.

INDIAN
TERRITORY

TEXAS

L. Superior

WIS.

IOWA

Missouri R.

Dubuque

Cedar Rapids

MICH.

L. Michigan

L. Huron

Milwaukee

Chicago

Detroit

ILL.

Springfield

Kansas R. St. Joseph

St. Louis

MO.

Cairo

Columbus

Paducah

Memphis

Arkansas R.

ARK.

Corinth

Decatur

MISS.

Vicksburg   Jackson

Montgomery

Pearl R.

LA.

Houston

Galveston

New Orleans

Mobile

Ft. Wayne

Indianapolis

IND.

Louisville

Ohio R.

Cincinnati

Toledo

Cleveland

OHIO

Columbus

Pittsburgh

KY.

Cumberland R.

Tennessee R.

Nashville

TENN.

Knoxville

Chattanooga

Mississippi R.

ALA.

Atlanta

Augusta

Macon

GA.

Savannah

L. Erie

Buffalo

PA.

L. Ontario

St. Lawrence R.

N.H.   ME.

VT.

L. Champlain

Albany

N.Y.

Connecticut R.

Portland

MASS.

Boston

R.I.

CONN.

New York

N.J.

Philadelphia

Baltimore

DEL.

MD.

VA.

Charlottesville

Washington, D.C.

Richmond

Lynchburg

Norfolk

N.C.

Raleigh

Charlotte

S.C.

Columbia

Charleston

Wilmington

ATLANTIC OCEAN

FLA.

Jacksonville

GULF OF MEXICO

| | Railroads operating in 1850 |
| | Lines added, 1850–1861 |

0   100   200   300   400 Miles

0   100   200   300   400 Kilometers

Unit 13

Western Trails, to 1860

The vast spaces of the American West long beckoned the adventurous, the resourceful, and the desperate. Beginning in 1807, keelboats ferried fur trappers up the Missouri River to make their search for beaver in the Rockies and along the Columbia River. By the mid-1830s these mountain men had marked the overland trails that would lead pioneers to Oregon and California.

The trails west served different purposes. In 1821 an American trader set out on a commercial expedition from Franklin, Missouri, to Santa Fe. The trip took two months. Soon about 80 wagons were using the Santa Fe Trail each year to trade cloth, hardware, glass, and books in return for Mexican blankets, beaver, wool, mules, and Mexican silver coins. By 1860 the wagons on the trail each year numbered in the thousands.

Before the opening of the Sante Fe Trail, few Americans had entered the Southwest. By the 1830s traders had ventured beyond Santa Fe, in the process extending the trail into California, with branches reaching Los Angeles and San Diego. Important commercial relations developed between Mexico's vast northern territories and the United States.

In contrast to the Santa Fe Trail, which primarily served merchants, the Oregon and California trails carried settlers into the Far West. Missionaries numbered among the earliest to make the six-month, 2,000-mile journey for the purpose of settling in Oregon. Then in 1843, the first great wagon train was organized at Independence, Missouri. The trail crossed Kansas to the Platte River and followed that stream to Fort Laramie, the last military outpost on the trail. The wagons crossed the continental divide at South Pass and wound their way through the imposing Rockies to a point near the source of the Snake River and then into the Columbia River country. Travel on the Oregon Trail tested the limits of human endurance. Migrants might encounter prairie fires, rain, wind, sudden blizzards, and—far less often than Hollywood suggests—hostile Indians. Food, water, and wood were scarce. A wagon train could make fifteen or twenty miles a day—or none at all. During the 1840s perhaps 12,000 migrants traversed the length of the Oregon Trail.

In 1846 and 1847 Mormons, fleeing persecution in Illinois because of their religious beliefs, followed another route, the Mormon Trail, to the valley of the Great Salt Lake in Utah. The Church of Jesus Christ of Latter-Day Saints had been founded in 1830 by Joseph Smith. The new religion gained adherents and established a close-knit community that remained separate and apart from the "gentiles." To escape the hostility of their neighbors, the Mormons had moved several times before arriving in Illinois. In 1846 Brigham Young led almost the entire Mormon community across Iowa to the Council Bluffs on the Missouri River. The next year he sent a group to settle outside the United States in the Salt Lake basin in Mexican territory. It was an isolated region, sheltered on the east by the Wasatch Mountains and on the south and west by desert. But fresh water and good soil were available, and the Mormons built both a thriving city and an efficient irrigation system. When their lands were annexed by the United States, the Mormons at first tried unsuccessfully to organize their own state, which they called Deseret. In Utah today, the Mormon church remains a powerful religious and political force.

After the thrilling discovery of gold in California, thousands of gold seekers took an offshoot of the Oregon Trail through the Sierra Nevada to the California gold fields. Early in 1848, along California's American River about 40 miles from Sacramento, carpenters building a sawmill for

John Augustus Sutter uncovered a golden nugget. The mill construction was forgotten as workers turned to gold hunting. Within a short time, most of the 500 inhabitants of San Francisco had deserted the town to look for gold. In 1849, 80,000 people descended on California in the great Gold Rush. In the summer of 1850 alone, 55,000 gold seekers traveled into the area near Sutter's Fort. In 1850 California became a part of one of the most difficult controversies in the continuing conflict over slavery. The trails had led west, and California was ready for statehood.

A. Map Exercises

1. Travelers on the western trails often severely lacked wood and water. Using the maps in Part II on pages 14, 16, and 18, explain why this was so.

2. The Oregon Trail and the other routes to the West crossed the continental divide. What is the continental divide? Label it on the map.

3. Considerable distances separate the California Trail from the Old Spanish Trail, and that from the Emigrant Trail, sometimes called the Oxbow Route. Using the maps in Part II on pages 14, 16, and 18, explain why this is so.

4. The mountains and the rivers provided formidable obstacles for western travelers. The rivers are not named on the map. Label them.

5. The first trip in 1821 from Missouri along the Santa Fe Trail took two months. Follow the trail on the map, and estimate the distance and the rate of speed.

6. Locate and label Council Bluffs on the map. Why is it called by that name?

B. Further Exercises

1. Wagons used by western travelers had to be simple and sturdy. Investigate what kinds were used. How dependable were the wagons?

2. Voyagers had to organize the division of labor on a western expedition with care. In a one- to two-page paper, explore what roles were typically assigned to men, women, and children.

3. The trek of the Mormons from Illinois to Iowa and then to the Great Salt Lake is a story of considerable dramatic power. Investigate it. What geographic obstacles did the Mormons have to overcome? In a one- to two-page paper, describe the trek from the vantage point of one of the migrating Mormons.

4. Look at the map of interstate highways on page 65 of Volume 2. Are there any similarities between today's highway routes and the trails west before the Civil War?

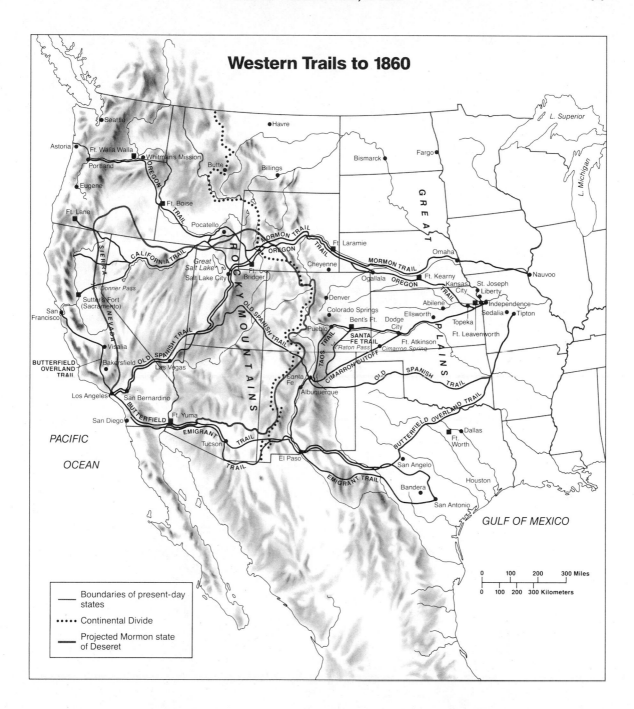

Western Trails to 1860

Boundaries of present-day states

•••• Continental Divide

Projected Mormon state of Deseret

Unit 14

Two Western Episodes: Tragedy and Triumph
The Donner Party, 1846–1847
The Pony Express, 1860–1861

The West was vast, its dangers were great, and most of those who crossed the plains, the mountains, and the deserts were inexperienced. The lure of the West was powerful as the attractions of California and Oregon were trumpeted far and wide. The Sacramento Valley and the Willamette Valley seemed virtual Edens to eager migrants from farther east. Many died along the way, but few parties of migrants suffered such travail as did the Donner party in 1846 and 1847.

George and Jacob Donner, wealthy Illinois farmers, were in their sixties when they organized a group headed for California and new opportunities. The members of the expedition were ill prepared for the journey, but the trip went well as far as Fort Bridger. Lansford Hastings, the author of the *Emigrants Guide to Oregon and California*, had written that travelers could save 400 miles by taking the Hastings Cutoff, which veered south of the Great Salt Lake. Hastings himself had never taken his own shortcut, but 87 of the original Donner party, including the Donner brothers themselves, were convinced and followed Hastings's advice. The others, heeding the warnings of veteran guides, continued on the trail to Fort Hall.

Travel on the new route was unremarkable at first, but the terrain soon became more and more difficult. Forward progress slowed as the expedition wandered in the Utah wilderness. At one point the emigrants spent 21 days traveling 36 miles. It was September 30 before they reached the well-marked California Trail on the Humboldt River. The group from which they separated at Fort Bridger had passed that point 45 days earlier.

The Donner party reached the eastern Sierra Nevada on October 28, and, tragically, they stopped to rest at Truckee Lake despite the lateness of the season. Early snow and five-foot drifts soon blocked their path as they tried to climb into the mountains. The members of the party built tents and covered them with clothing, blankets, and animal hides. The snow kept coming. Drifts reached 40 feet. Much of their livestock wandered off and perished. To survive, members of the group ate mice and even their shoes. In the end, the survivors escaped starvation only by cannibalizing those who died first.

In mid-December a group of 17 made a desperate effort to cross through Truckee Pass and find help. More than a month passed before seven badly frostbitten survivors reached an American settlement. Rescue parties went out to save those trapped near Truckee Pass. The situation they found was gruesome. Those still alive were half-crazed with hunger and exposure. Of the 87 original members of the Donner party who had chosen the "shortcut" to California, only 47 survived. A horrified nation was enthralled by accounts of the Donner tragedy in the penny press.

Despite disasters like that befalling the Donner group, the western population increased through the influx of midwestern and eastern migrants, and the demand for improved communication grew steadily. In 1857, the postmaster general called for bids on a fast and continuous service to the West Coast by road. The Butterfield Overland Stage Company won the contract as well as a federal subsidy of $600,000 a year. Other companies appeared from time to time, and

73

some also gained United States mail contracts. It was the company of Russell, Majors & Waddell that dramatically sped up the trip by introducing the pony express.

Public announcement of the pony express created a sensation. Russell advertised that he would transport letters between St. Joseph, Missouri, and Placerville, California, at $5 an ounce and that he would do it in ten days, half of Butterfield's best time. (Later the rate decreased to $1 a half-ounce.) There was considerable doubt as to whether such speed was possible, particularly in winter. Service began on April 3, 1860, when the first rider left St. Joseph. The next day a rider set out east from Sacramento. The first trip was made in ten and a half days.

The route ran 1,966 miles from St. Joseph to Sacramento, and much depended on the skill and endurance of the riders. Eighty were employed, half going east and half going west. Small men and boys were chosen, and the weight of their clothes and equipment kept to a minimum. The mail was wrapped in oiled silk to protect it from the weather. Generally, 40 to 90 letters were carried each trip. Riders normally rode 60 or 70 miles but could cover 100 miles if necessary. Relay stations to supply fresh horses were located about ten miles apart. Riders made the round trip twice a week. When any were struck by sickness or accident, others doubled their runs. For this arduous work—for fast riding on bad roads in all kinds of weather—the men ordinarily earned about $125 a month.

The real test of the pony express came in the winter of 1860–1861. Although cold and snow slowed them down, the men continued to ride through. In the spring of 1861, they were averaging nine days for the trip. In its 16 months of operation, pony express riders traveled 650,000 miles and lost only one shipment. They successfully delivered 35,000 pieces of mail.

Pony express service ended only a short time after it had begun, giving way to the telegraph. The first telegraph line across the plains and the mountains was completed in October 1861. No longer was there any reason for the existence of a pony express. Technology had displaced it.

A. Map Exercises

1. The map lays out the routes of the Donner party and the pony express. The map does not reveal the names of the present-day states through which the routes passed. Write them in.

2. The fording of rivers was ever a problem for western travelers. On the maps mark all the fords that you can observe. Consider the numerous smaller but still difficult streams that the map does not reveal.

3. Someone with a map and a ruler might try to save many miles by drawing a route directly from St. Joseph to Sacramento. What obstacles make such a route impossible?

4. The speed of the pony express was its most remarkable feature. If a wagon train traveled at, say, fifteen miles a day, how long would it take to cross Kansas? Texas?

5. What was the rate of speed of the pony express per day? Per hour? Remember that the trail was not lit at night.

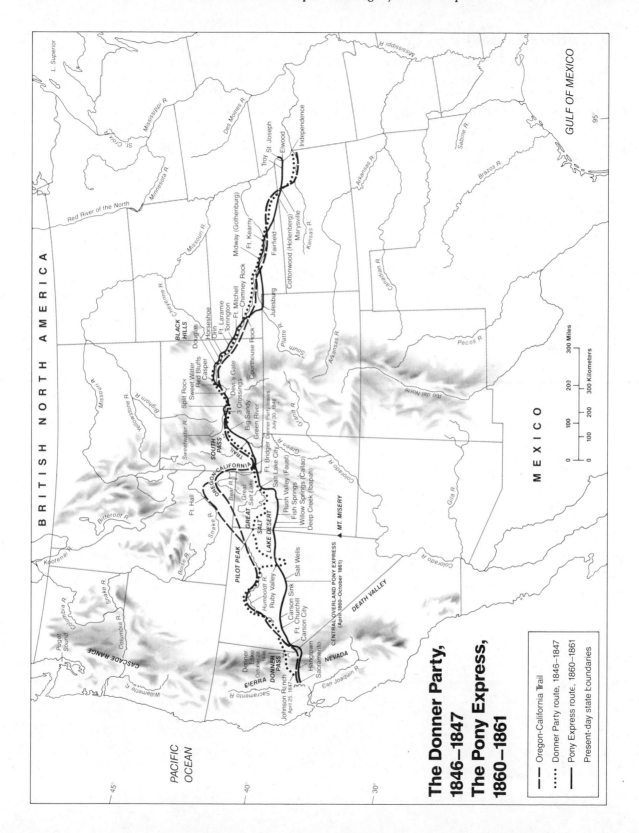

The Donner Party, 1846–1847
The Pony Express, 1860–1861

- — — Oregon-California Trail
- ·········· Donner Party route, 1846–1847
- ——— Pony Express route, 1860–1861
- ———— Present-day state boundaries

B. Further Exercises

1. One of the early snows in Yellowstone Park in Wyoming once closed the roads on August 25. Those who were trapped, facing no real danger, simply celebrated an early Christmas. The Donner party also were trapped by an early snowfall. What is the earliest significant snowfall recorded in the Rocky Mountain states? In the Sierra Nevada?

2. The Western Trails, to 1860, map on page 71 shows the Butterfield Route to have gone much farther south than did the pony express. Should Butterfield have tried a central route also, even though coaches rather than ponies were used?

3. Travelers in the West were always trying to improve their situation. Using the maps in Part II on pages 12, 14, 16, and 18, construct an alternative to the central route of the pony express and the southern route used by Butterfield.

4. Only two years after the Donner episode, another disaster occurred, this time in Death Valley. Research the story of the Jayhawkers and their tragedy, and write a one- to two-page paper summarizing what happened. Trace the Jayhawkers' route on the map.

Unit 15

The Texas Revolution of 1836
and the Mexican War, 1846–1848

For many years the vast northern reaches of New Spain were relatively unpopulated by Europeans. In the eighteenth century the Spanish, to strengthen their control of California and expand their missionary efforts, encouraged the Franciscan order to build a chain of missions along the California coast from San Diego to San Francisco.

In 1821 a Mexican revolution against Spain succeeded. Independence brought major changes to the northern provinces—California, New Mexico, Arizona, and Texas. In California the mission system went into decline. Many Mexicans in California wanted the missions to be secularized, and their vast properties divided. The government drove out the Franciscan friars, and within a short time the mission properties had for the most part passed into the hands of a group of wealthy landowners. In New Mexico and Arizona the collapse of Spanish authority allowed American traders and trappers into the area. In Texas, Mexican independence opened the way for American adventurers and settlers.

By 1830 the Mexican government was becoming alarmed at the tenuousness of its control over Texas. As the ruling regime tried to prohibit the further immigration of Americans and to prevent the further importation of slaves, tensions rose. Mexican president Santa Anna succeeded in instituting constitutional reform to increase central authority and decrease regional power. In response, the Texans proclaimed their independence. When Santa Anna's army destroyed a small band of Texas rebels at the Alamo mission in San Antonio, the American press cried out for revenge. Texas general Sam Houston, with a force of nearly 800 men, crushed the Mexican army at San Jacinto and captured Santa Anna.

Texas remained an independent republic for nine years. Its efforts to join the United States were mired in controversy over the extension of slavery. When the United States finally annexed Texas in 1845, Mexico broke off diplomatic relations. Mexican nationalists considered Texas a stolen province and resented the claim that Texas extended south to the Rio Grande. Under Spanish rule the Nueces River had marked the southern boundary, and it was only in 1836, while Santa Anna was held captive, that he agreed to the Rio Grande as a condition of his release. The Mexican government repudiated the agreement.

American expansionists and advocates of Manifest Destiny had long been trying to obtain from Mexico what is now the Southwest of the United States—by money if possible, by force if necessary. When President James Polk's peaceful efforts failed, he ordered General Zachary Taylor to march to the Rio Grande. American cannon were soon trained on Matamoros, across the river. It was here that hostilities began.

Mexico entered the war with a will. The Mexicans had concluded that nothing short of war would stop Yankee aggression. Confident of victory because of their large army, they felt ready. But their weapons were outdated, their supplies limited, and their leadership inept. There were three major campaigns. General Taylor pushed south into Mexico. Colonel Stephen W. Kearny moved west to Santa Fe as American settlers in California declared their independence from Mexico. General Winfield Scott landed near Vera Cruz and marched to victory at Mexico City.

By the Treaty of Guadalupe Hidalgo (1848), the United States obtained New Mexico, California, and Texas (with the Rio Grande boundary) for $15 million and the assumption of claims held by United States citizens against Mexico. Having gained possession of more than a half million square miles of territory, the United States became a power on the Pacific. And it acquired a grudging neighbor that had lost half its territory to American military might and that nursed its resentment with cherished stories of resistance like that of the five *niños héroes*, the child heroes, military cadets who gave their lives in defense of Chapultepec, just outside Mexico City. The United States also acquired a sizable non-Protestant, only partially European minority at a time when respect for ethnic and cultural minorities was not part of societal thinking—a minority whose claims for justice were only beginning to be listened to a century later.

A. Map Exercises

1. In 1847 Congressman Abraham Lincoln of Illinois, speaking in opposition to the Mexican War, demanded to be shown the "particular spot" where American blood had been shed on American soil to start the fighting. Find the "particular spot" on the map. Did it in fact lie on American soil?

2. Note the size of the area in dispute between Texas and Mexico. The Texans claimed the Rio Grande as their boundary all the way to its source. What present-day states are included in the disputed area? List four cities or towns within it.

3. Consult the physiographic and rainfall maps in Part II on pages 14 and 18. Write a brief description of the disputed region by using the information that the maps reveal.

4. On the map of the Texas Revolution and the Mexican War, follow the three major campaign routes in the war. Mark Taylor's advance to Monterrey, Kearny's advance to Santa Fe and the coast, and Scott's advance to Vera Cruz and to Mexico City.

B. Further Exercises

1. One of the early foundations of Spanish power in California was the mission system. On the map locate and name five of the missions.

2. Note the names Rio Grande on the north side of the river and Rio Bravo del Norte on the south. Why are there two names?

3. Alexander Doniphan, John C. Frémont, and John D. Sloat played important roles in the Mexican War. Research their military activities, and trace their advances on the map.

4. The story of the *niños héroes* of Chapultepec is well known to Mexicans. Mexican city maps reveal that many cities have a street named after the *niños héroes*. What does this fact suggest about Mexican attitudes toward the war?

5. Two of the most colorful characters in all of history were Sam Houston and Antonio López de Santa Anna. Their careers are worth investigating. Write a one-page biographical sketch of each man. Note Goliad and San Jacinto on the map. What happened there to Santa Anna and Houston?

**The Texas Revolution
of 1836 and the
Mexican War, 1846–1848**

OREGON
COUNTRY

UNORGANIZED
TERRITORY

IOWA

U N I T E D   S T A T E S

MISSOURI

Ft. Leavenworth

Missouri R.

Kearny

ARKANSAS

Sonoma
(Bear Flag Revolt)
June 14, 1846

San Francisco
occupied
July 10, 1846

Monterey
occupied July 7, 1846

Frémont

Colorado R.

San Gabriel
Jan. 8, 1847

Los
Angeles

San Pasqual
Dec. 6, 1846

San Diego

Santa Fe
occupied Aug. 18, 1846

U.S. Navy

Kearny

DISPUTED
AREA

TEXAS

San Antonio
Alamo March 1836

Austin

San Jacinto
April 1836

LOUISIANA

Houston

New Orleans

PACIFIC
OCEAN

M E X I C O

Guaymas

Rio Grande
Rio Bravo del Norte

Nueces R.

Goliad

Scott

Santa Anna

Chihuahua

Doniphan

Monterrey
Sept. 21–24,
1846

Palo Alto
May 8, 1846

Matamoros

Mississippi R.

Sloat 1846

Blockade

Buena Vista
Feb. 22–23, 1847

Taylor

GULF OF MEXICO

0   100   200   300   400 Miles

0   100   200   300   400 Kilometers

Mazatlán

Santa Anna

Tampico
occupied
Nov. 14, 1846

Blockade

Cerro Gordo
April 18, 1847

Mexico City
Sept. 13–14, 1847

Vera Cruz
occupied March 29, 1847

Scott

Sloat

Capture of Mexico City
September 1847

Guadalupe
Hidalgo

L.
Texcoco

Chapultepec
Sept. 13

Mexico City occupied Sept. 14

San Angel

Churubusco Aug. 20

San Antonio

L.
Xochimilco

L.
Chalco

Taylor

Buena
Vista

Padierna
Aug. 18

San
Gregorio

Ayocingo

0   5   10 Miles

0   5   10 Kilometers

Legend:
← Texan or American forces
◄--- Mexican forces
□ Texan or American victories
○ Mexican victories
— Boundary of territory ceded by Mexico, 1848
† Mission stations in California

Unit 16

The Missouri Compromise of 1820
The Compromise of 1850
The Kansas-Nebraska Act, 1854
Bleeding Kansas

An undercurrent of sectional rivalry characterized the United States from its beginnings, but following the War of 1812, the potential for serious sectional dispute became more and more visible beneath a surface appearance of national good feeling. No issue was more divisive than slavery. It had been a subject of controversy as early as the Constitutional Convention of 1787, where it was papered over by the three-fifths compromise. The slave states had wanted the slave population counted for purposes of congressional representation but not taxation. The reverse was true on the part of delegates from the North. Agreement was finally reached to count free persons for both purposes as well as "three-fifths of all other persons." The word "slave" was carefully avoided.

Before 1820 five additional slave states were admitted to the Union. The Senate was in balance: eleven free states and eleven slave states. In the Northwest Ordinance of 1787, Congress had limited slavery north of the Ohio River while allowing it in the South. In 1819, however, the territory of Missouri petitioned for admission as a slave state. It was generally understood that what happened to Missouri would affect the future of slavery beyond the Mississippi.

Southerners insisted that new states had the same sovereign rights as did the old. Congress, they believed, could not make the abolition of slavery a condition of admission to the Union. Northerners replied that Congress had full authority over the territories and that the Founding Fathers had not intended slavery to spread into the West. Political as well as constitutional issues formed a part of the debate. By 1819 the population of the free states had given them a majority of 105 to 81 in the House of Representatives. Southerners sought some compensation in the Senate. Southerners also accused the moribund Federalist party of deliberately stirring up trouble in order to win popular support in the North.

The settlement of the Missouri question did not end the controversy over the future of slavery. That problem was just put off by a compromise fashioned largely by Representative Henry Clay of Kentucky. By its terms, Missouri gained admission as a slave state, and, to keep the Senate in balance, Maine entered as a free state. The remaining territory of the Louisiana Purchase was divided along the line 36° 30′ north latitude. North of that line, except for Missouri, slavery was to be "forever prohibited."

* * * *

By 1850 the vast territory of the Mexican cession had been added to the United States, and a rush of more than 80,000 gold seekers made California eligible for admission to the Union. The government had to consider the future of slavery in these new lands. Free-soilers wanted to prohibit slavery. Proslavery forces argued that not only did Congress lack the constitutional right to exclude slavery from the territories, but it also had a positive duty to protect the property—

including the slave property—of those who lived there. The longer the Mexican cession territory was left unorganized, the greater would be the friction between these opposed points of view.

There were other problems to deal with as well. The boundary between Texas and New Mexico was in dispute. The very size of the Texas claim raised northern fears that Texas might be divided to form several slave states. Abolitionists were gaining support in the North for their demand that slavery be abolished in the District of Columbia. Southerners resented the lack of enforcement of the Fugitive Slave Act of 1793 and called for more effective legislation. Feelings ran high, and relations were tense as the Great Compromiser, Henry Clay, sought to fashion a comprehensive settlement of all outstanding issues with a so-called omnibus bill. Congress debated his proposals for more than seven months, with moderates under constant attack from proslavery and antislavery opponents of compromise. The moderates developed an effective political technique to win the day. If each section of the proposed bill were taken up separately, the moderates could gain the votes of those who opposed the compromise as a whole but favored individual parts. Senator Stephen A. Douglas of Illinois replaced Clay in the leadership role, and by September 1850 all of the omnibus bill's measures had been passed: (1) California entered the Union as a free state, upsetting the balance in the Senate 16 to 15. (2) The territories of New Mexico and Utah were created from the rest of the Mexican cession, with no restriction on slavery. The people of those territories were to exercise "popular sovereignty" and decide for themselves. (3) The boundary of Texas was fixed as it exists today, and the federal government compensated Texas with $10 million. (4) The slave trade, but not slavery itself, was abolished in the District of Columbia. (5) A more rigorous Fugitive Slave Act replaced the old one.

The sectional dispute over slavery was stilled for the moment, but the controversy had far from ended.

* * * *

The Kansas-Nebraska Act of 1854 was an effort to organize the West and to advance the career of its sponsor, Stephen A. Douglas of Illinois, the chairman of the Senate committee on territories. Douglas was eager to organize the plains, to drive out the Indians, and to lay the basis for a transcontinental railroad with an eastern terminus at Chicago. But the proponents of a rail line running to St. Louis were also hard at work, and the southern proponents of a New Orleans terminus had already persuaded the United States to purchase land south of the Gila River as a site for a potential southern route.

Douglas hoped that his efforts to open the West would win him the Democratic nomination for the presidency, but he also recognized that his bill would fail without southern support. In its text he used the identical language regarding the future of slavery that had been employed in the Utah and New Mexico acts of 1850—wording that permitted popular sovereignty. Douglas's bill was intended to supersede the prohibition of slavery north of 36° 30′, but southerners were not satisfied. They wanted specific repeal of the Missouri Compromise. Douglas agreed, reasoning that the climate and soil of the prairie in Kansas and Nebraska would not support slavery-based agriculture anyway. He could win southern support, he thought, without also getting slavery.

Douglas failed to understand how much slavery had become a moral issue. He was feared and distrusted both by proslavery planters who refused to commit the future of slavery to popular sovereignty and by leaders of the antislavery movement. Nevertheless, the Kansas-Nebraska Act passed, and two territories were created, each to be organized immediately on the basis of popular sovereignty. Nebraska seemed destined to be a free state. Kansas, immediately west of Missouri, was another matter.

* * * *

Kansas soon exploded into a battleground between free-soilers (also called free-staters) and proslavery forces. The Emigrant Aid Society in Massachusetts recruited and sent more than 1,200 New England free-soilers to Kansas. But most of the Kansas settlers came—as was typical when a new territory was opened—from neighboring states. A majority were free-soilers, but many hailed from Missouri. Although the slaveholders among them were few, the nonslaveholders also objected to abolitionism.

Kansas held its first election for a territorial legislature in March 1855. Some 5,000 Missourians—who were not Kansas residents—crossed the state line to cast illegal ballots. Many came armed and their fraudulent vote prevailed. The new proslavery Kansas legislature established itself at Lecompton, expelled antislavery members, and drew up a slave code. Antislavery Kansans were unwilling to accept the situation. Denouncing the election fraud, free-soilers held their own constitutional convention and created a free-soil government at Topeka. Far from seeking racial harmony, it banned blacks from the state altogether. Free soil was for whites only. Kansas now had two governments.

Civil war in Kansas was not long in coming. In 1856 a mob smashed the presses of a free-soil newspaper in Lawrence and destroyed homes and shops there. Three days later, John Brown murdered five men near Pottawatomie Creek, using specially sharpened broadswords to do, he believed, God's work. Missourians retaliated by burning the free-state town of Osawatomie. A brutal guerrilla war over the summer left more than 200 dead. Order was not restored until federal troops arrived in September 1856. Although hostilities subsided, the question of slavery in Kansas and the other territories was far from settled.

A. Map Exercises

1. Six slave and seven free states had made up the original thirteen. List their names. Prior to the outbreak of controversy over the admission of Missouri, nine more states—five slave and four free—had been added to the Union. Which were they?

2. In 1850 some northerners feared that Texas, with its extensive claims to territory, might be divided into several slave states. Examine the map of The Texas Revolution of 1836 and the Mexican War, 1846–1848, on page 79, and sketch on the map of the Compromise of 1850 the extent of the Texas claim. Estimate the size of the portion that went to the New Mexico Territory in the settlement.

3. The proposed Mormon state of Deseret was also quite large. Look at the map of Western Trails, to 1860, on page 71. Sketch in Deseret on the map of the Compromise of 1850. What proportion of the Utah and New Mexico territories did it include?

4. In 1853 the United States bought from Mexico a parcel of land south of the Gila River known as the Gadsden Purchase. Consult the Political Map of the United States on page 12 and use it to draw in the Gadsden Purchase on the map of the Compromise of 1850 and the Kansas-Nebraska Act, 1854.

5. The map of Bleeding Kansas shows several rivers. To help fix location in mind, label the rivers. Write in the latitude and longitude of Missouri's southern boundary.

6. The Bleeding Kansas map shows Missouri, the Kansas Territory, the Nebraska Territory, and a fourth area. What is the name of the fourth area?

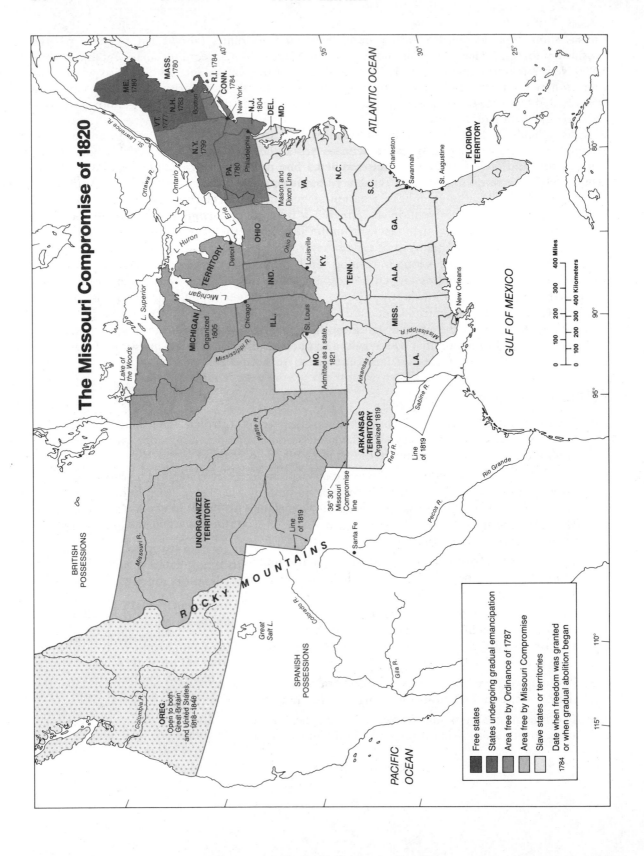

The Missouri Compromise of 1820

ATLANTIC OCEAN

St. Lawrence R.

Ottawa R.

L. Ontario

L. Erie

L. Huron

L. Superior

Lake of the Woods

MASS. 1780

ME. 1780

N.H. 1783

R.I. 1784

CONN. 1784

VT. 1777

N.Y. 1799

N.J. 1804

DEL.

MD.

PA. 1780

Boston

New York

Philadelphia

Mason and Dixon Line

VA.

N.C.

S.C.

GA.

Charleston

Savannah

St. Augustine

FLORIDA TERRITORY

OHIO

IND.

ILL.

MICHIGAN TERRITORY Organized 1805

Detroit

L. Michigan

Chicago

Ohio R.

Louisville

KY.

TENN.

ALA.

MISS.

LA.

MO. Admitted as a state, 1821

St. Louis

Mississippi R.

New Orleans

GULF OF MEXICO

ARKANSAS TERRITORY Organized 1819

Arkansas R.

Red R.

Sabine R.

Line of 1819

36° 30' Missouri Compromise line

Line of 1819

UNORGANIZED TERRITORY

Missouri R.

Platte R.

Santa Fe

ROCKY MOUNTAINS

Rio Grande

Pecos R.

Gila R.

Colorado R.

Great Salt L.

Columbia R.

OREG: Open to both Great Britain and United States, 1818-1846

BRITISH POSSESSIONS

SPANISH POSSESSIONS

PACIFIC OCEAN

400 Miles

400 Kilometers

0 100 200 300

40°

35°

30°

25°

80°

90°

95°

110°

115°

Free states

States undergoing gradual emancipation

Area free by Ordinance of 1787

Area free by Missouri Compromise

Slave states or territories

1784 Date when freedom was granted or when gradual abolition began

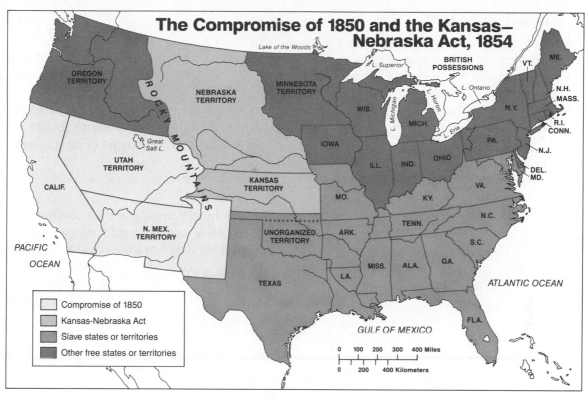

The Compromise of 1850 and the Kansas–Nebraska Act, 1854

Lake of the Woods

BRITISH
POSSESSIONS

VT.
ME.

L. Superior
L. Ontario

OREGON
TERRITORY

MINNESOTA
TERRITORY

N.H.
MASS.

NEBRASKA
TERRITORY

WIS.

L. Michigan

L. Huron

N.Y.

R.I.
CONN.

IOWA

MICH.

L. Erie

PA.

N.J.

Great
Salt L.

UTAH
TERRITORY

ILL.

IND.

OHIO

DEL.
MD.

CALIF.

KANSAS
TERRITORY

MO.

VA.

KY.

N. MEX.
TERRITORY

UNORGANIZED
TERRITORY

ARK.

TENN.

N.C.

PACIFIC
OCEAN

S.C.

MISS.

ALA.

GA.

TEXAS

LA.

ATLANTIC OCEAN

FLA.

GULF OF MEXICO

ROCKY MOUNTAINS

0   100   200   300   400 Miles

0   200   400 Kilometers

Legend:
- Compromise of 1850
- Kansas-Nebraska Act
- Slave states or territories
- Other free states or territories

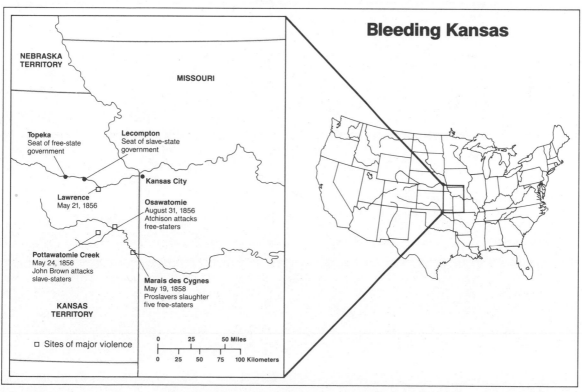

Bleeding Kansas

NEBRASKA
TERRITORY

MISSOURI

Topeka
Seat of free-state
government

Lecompton
Seat of slave-state
government

● **Kansas City**

Lawrence
May 21, 1856

Osawatomie
August 31, 1856
Atchison attacks
free-staters

Pottawatomie Creek
May 24, 1856
John Brown attacks
slave-staters

Marais des Cygnes
May 19, 1858
Proslavers slaughter
five free-staters

KANSAS
TERRITORY

□ Sites of major violence

0   25   50 Miles

0   25   50   75   100 Kilometers

B. Further Exercises

1. The Compromise of 1820 and the Compromise of 1850 are two of the more famous compromises in United States history. Compromise avoids confrontation. But is it always appropriate? Were these both alternatives in 1820 and 1850? Write a one- to two-page essay on the question.

2. The geography of Kansas and Nebraska, Senator Douglas believed, would be hostile to the spread of slavery. Was he correct? Is slavery governed by geographic conditions?

3. The Missouri Compromise's fixing of the line of division at 36° 30′ north latitude suggests the importance of this method of measuring space on the surface of a sphere. What important line was drawn at 49°N.? At what line of latitude is your college or university? At what line of longitude?

Unit 17

Secession and the Civil War

In the election of 1860, the national popular vote was divided among four candidates for president. Although Abraham Lincoln received only 40 percent of the national total, he swept the electoral votes, winning every free state while losing every slave state. With Lincoln's election, the South's worst fears had been realized. The election proved that voters in the North were numerous enough to give national power to a minority party, one without southern support. Slaveowners' fears were not eased by Lincoln's assurances regarding the constitutional protection of slavery in the existing states. If the Republican Party should decide to move further along a path hostile to slavery, the South would be unable to check it.

South Carolina planned a secession convention for January 1861, but when extremists forced the issue, a special convention on December 20, 1860, repealed the state's ratification of the Constitution and withdrew South Carolina from the Union. In the other southern states, discussion turned on whether to secede immediately or wait until Lincoln had shown his hand. By the beginning of February 1861, secessionists had won the day in six more states. Delegates of the seceded states adopted a constitution for the Confederate States of America on February 7, 1861.

On March 4 Abraham Lincoln took his oath of office as the sixteenth president of the United States. In his inaugural message, Lincoln said that he would support the Union by maintaining possession of federal property in the South. The seceded states, however, had taken control of all federal installations within their borders with the exception of Fort Sumter in Charleston Harbor, South Carolina, and Fort Pickens at Pensacola, Florida. Earlier in the year, federal efforts to supply Fort Sumter had been repulsed by shore batteries. Now, on the day after his inauguration, Lincoln learned that Sumter would have to be abandoned within six weeks if it failed to receive additional provisions. Fort Sumter had no special military value, but its symbolic value was enormous. Provoking a confrontation by use of force at the very center of secessionist sentiment might drive the border states to secede. On the other hand, evacuating Sumter would be a blow to Union pride. Lincoln notified South Carolina's governor that, although he would not resort to force of arms unless driven to it, he would provision Fort Sumter. South Carolina responded by demanding the withdrawal of federal troops. Knowing that help for Sumter was on the way, South Carolina's batteries began firing on the fort at 4:30 A.M., April 12, 1861. On April 13, Sumter surrendered. The Civil War had begun.

By late May four more states voted to leave the Union. The Confederacy now numbered eleven states with a population of nearly 9 million people, including 3.5 million slaves. Four slaveholding border states, with their 23 million people, remained in the Union.

Both the North and the South believed that the war could be quickly won. In July 1861, at the first battle of Bull Run (First Manassas), 20 miles south of Washington, sightseers came to observe the fighting as though at a tournament. The brutal reality of war soon put an end to such folly. General George B. McClellan was given command of the Army of the Potomac. His Peninsula Campaign (March to July 1862) was an unsuccessful effort to advance on the Confederate capital at Richmond. General Robert E. Lee took command of the southern troops. In the West, Union forces under the command of General Ulysses S. Grant defeated the Confederates at Fort Donelson but were stopped at Shiloh in April 1862. In September of that year, McClellan and the Union won in the bloody engagements at Antietam (Sharpsburg) in Maryland but lost the opportunity of decisively defeating the Confederates. Lincoln replaced McClellan.

Early in the war, Lincoln had implemented a blockade of the southern Atlantic coast. The Confederates attempted to break the blockade with the frigate *Merrimac*, which had been reconstructed as an ironclad. In March 1862 the *Merrimac* fought the Union ironclad, *Monitor*, to a draw. The South never again challenged U.S. naval supremacy. The days of wooden ships were numbered.

Lincoln had tried to avoid the issue of slavery as long as any possibility remained that the border states might join the Confederacy. After Antietam, however, he issued a preliminary emancipation proclamation, declaring that on January 1, 1863, in every part of the South still in rebellion, all slaves would be "thenceforward and forever free."

Until the middle of 1863, it still seemed possible that the South could emerge victorious. If Lee could take the war to the North, he might threaten Washington, destroy northern morale, and force a negotiated peace. Lee reached Gettysburg, Pennsylvania, but was driven back in bloody fighting. The defeat at Gettysburg coincided with Grant's capture of Vicksburg, a key southern port on the Mississippi. With Confederate forces in the West now split in half, Grant was called on to assume command of all northern troops. In the spring of 1864, he pressed a campaign to advance on Richmond. The cost was tremendous, but the North could draw on reserves that the South did not have. In September 1864 Union general William Tecumseh Sherman captured Atlanta, a major rail center, and cut a ruinous swath across Georgia to the sea. By April 1865 northern pressure in Virginia had become irresistible. On April 9 Lee surrendered at Appomattox Court House. The tragic war between brothers was over.

A. Map Exercises

1. South Carolina was the first state to secede. Mark it on the map with the numeral 1. By February 1861 there was a second wave of six seceding states. Mark them with the numeral 2, and list their names. Note that all are contiguous and all are in the Deep South. In April and May four more states seceded. Mark them with the numeral 3, and add their names to the list. Four slaveholding border states stayed with the Union. Mark them with the label "Union-slave," and list their names as well.

2. The Peninsula Campaign took place in the region near the James and York rivers. Examine the map, and give the reason for the name. Mark the engagements as one of the first major campaigns of the war.

3. The battle of the ironclads took place at Hampton Roads, not far from Norfolk, Virginia. Mark the spot as one of the war's major naval engagements. What does "roads" mean at sea?

4. In examining the map of the war's major battles, note that almost all the fighting took place within the Confederate states. What effect did that fact have on supply lines to the Northern and Southern forces? On destruction of homes and property? On feelings of resentment after the war?

5. Reread the statement about the Emancipation Proclamation. Mark the areas on the map, if any, in which the Emancipation Proclamation brought freedom to slaves.

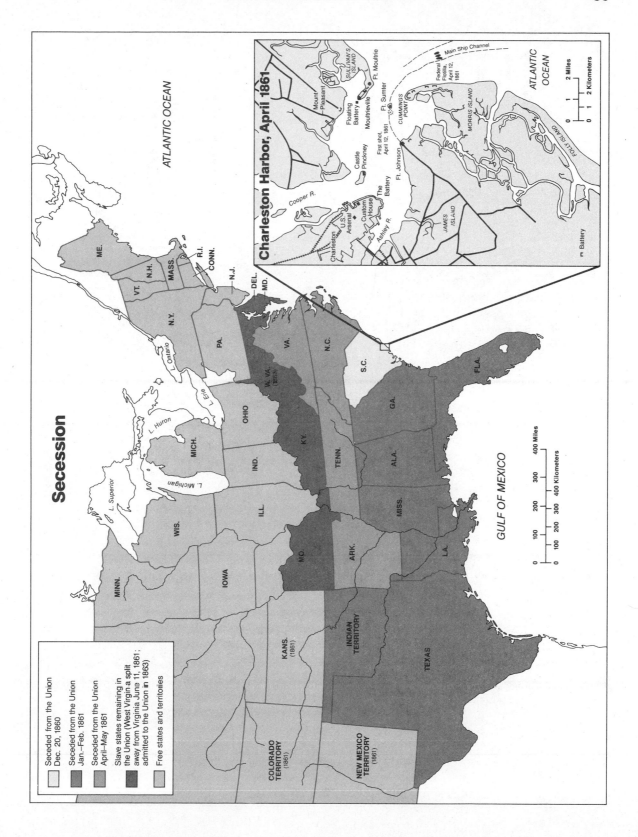

Secession

Charleston Harbor, April 1861

ATLANTIC OCEAN

GULF OF MEXICO

Legend:
- Seceded from the Union Dec. 20, 1860
- Seceded from the Union Jan.–Feb. 1861
- Seceded from the Union April–May 1861
- Slave states remaining in the Union (West Virginia a split away from Virginia June 11, 1861; admitted to the Union in 1863)
- Free states and territories

MINN.
WIS.
IOWA
ILL.
IND.
OHIO
MICH.
ME.
N.H.
VT.
MASS.
R.I.
CONN.
N.Y.
PA.
N.J.
DEL.
MD.
VA.
W. VA. (1863)
KY.
TENN.
N.C.
S.C.
GA.
FLA.
ALA.
MISS.
ARK.
LA.
MO.
KANS. (1861)
TEXAS
INDIAN TERRITORY
COLORADO TERRITORY (1861)
NEW MEXICO TERRITORY (1861)

L. Superior
L. Michigan
L. Huron
L. Erie
L. Ontario

0 100 200 300 400 Miles
0 100 200 300 400 Kilometers

Charleston Harbor inset:
Main Ship Channel
ATLANTIC OCEAN
SULLIVAN'S ISLAND
Ft. Moultrie
Mount Pleasant
Floating Battery
Moultrieville
Ft. Sumter
Federal Flotilla, April 12, 1861
CUMMINGS POINT
MORRIS ISLAND
First shot, April 12, 1861
Ft. Johnson
Castle Pinckney
Cooper R.
The Battery
Custom House
U.S. Arsenal
Charleston
Ashley R.
JAMES ISLAND
FOLLY ISLAND
Battery

0 1 2 Miles
0 1 2 Kilometers

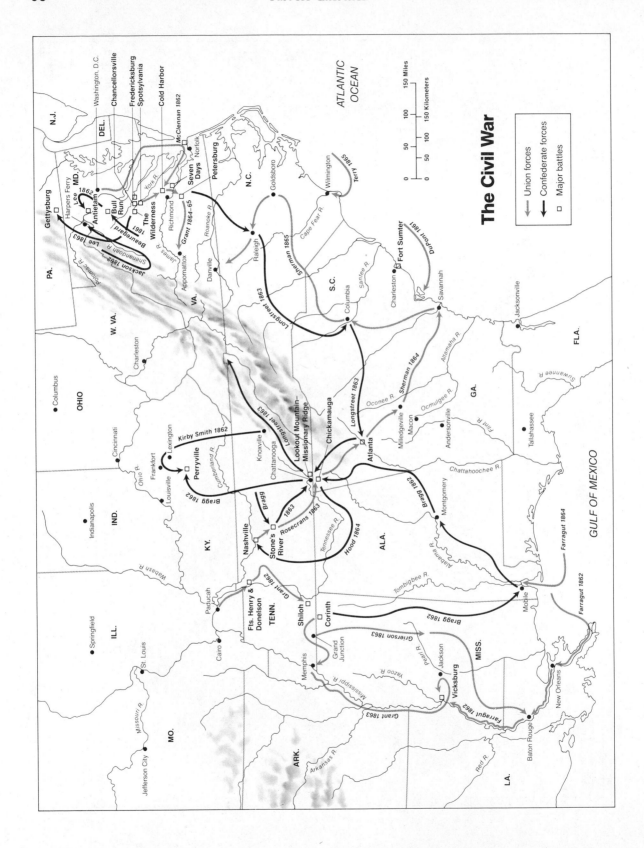

The Civil War

→ Union forces
→ Confederate forces
□ Major battles

B. Further Exercises

1. Obtain a state-by-state distribution of votes in the presidential election of 1860. Compare it with the map of states seceding from the Union. Can you discern a pattern of relationship? Explain.

2. The map reveals that Fort Sumter is on an island in Charleston Harbor. If Sumter had been on the mainland, what effect might such a location have had on the beginning of the Civil War?

3. The first Confederate capital was at Montgomery, Alabama. Mark that city on the map. The second capital was at Richmond, Virginia. Mark that city as well. Look into why the capital was transferred, and write a one- to two-page paper discussing the reasons for the relocation and the character of Richmond during the war.

4. Look again at the war map, and note four major regions: Virginia-Maryland, Kentucky-Tennessee, Mississippi, and Georgia-South Carolina. Read about a major battle in each of the four regions, and add symbols to the map or draw the detail on a separate sheet to show the development of the battle for one of them. Create a symbol for the Confederate forces and one for the Union forces. Try to show the positions of the troops and the progress of the fighting by drawing arrows.

5. Atlanta became a focus of attack because it was a rail center. Why did that fact make it important? Had rail centers ever been strategic objectives in earlier wars? Why or why not?

6. Question 5 on page 88 asks for designation of the area in which slaves were freed by the Emancipation Proclamation. Why did President Lincoln issue the proclamation?

Unit 18

Reconstruction, 1865 –1877

Even while the Civil War was still raging, the presence of federal troops in occupied Tennessee, Arkansas, and Louisiana enabled President Lincoln to name military governors for these states as early as 1862. He also began plans for installing non-Confederate civilian state governments when as few as 10 percent of the voters (as of 1860) were willing to support Union authority. Radical Republicans in Congress, however, were outraged by the president's softness in punishing rebellion, his inadequate protection of the freedmen, and his failure to use the opportunity to strengthen the Republican party. The plan permitted the continuance of pre-war state constitutions and legal codes, omitted any requirement that freedmen should be given civil rights, and allowed a small nucleus of loyal citizens, regardless of party affiliation, to secure control.

Lincoln's "Ten Percent" plan was extremely lenient. Despite four years of brutal and bloody war, the president looked for no punishment, no retribution. "I think it is enough," he said, if a man "does no wrong hereafter." After Lincoln's assassination in April 1865, President Andrew Johnson appointed a provisional governor for each of the former Confederate states except those that had already met Lincoln's requirements. All were obliged to call conventions to adopt the Thirteenth Amendment ending slavery, nullify or repeal their ordinances of secession, and repudiate state debts created by the war. By early 1866 each of the states that once formed the Confederacy had followed Johnson's instructions and were recognized by the president. Each state acknowledged the end of slavery, but none made a concession toward enabling blacks to vote.

Congress held the view that directing Reconstruction was properly a congressional, not a presidential, function. Moreover, certain aspects of the Johnson governments angered northern Republicans. Those regimes frequently were led by former Confederates who had received pardons from President Johnson. And as far as blacks were concerned, southern states not only refused to give freedmen the vote but also resisted other changes. While blacks were technically free, whites expected them to work and live as they had before emancipation. To this end, the new southern state governments enacted a series of black codes to provide a means of racial control and to fashion a labor system as close to slavery as possible.

In 1866 Congress established the Joint Committee on Reconstruction and proposed the Fourteenth Amendment, defining citizenship as including blacks and guaranteeing that the states could not take away individual rights. Congress made the amendment's ratification a condition for a state's readmission to the Union. That same year, the Republicans won a three-to-one majority in Congress and in the following year, enacted, over Johnson's veto, two Reconstruction Acts, declaring Johnson's governments in the South invalid and dividing the South into five military districts, each to be supervised by a general and subject to martial law. New state constitutions were to be prepared, specifying that blacks must be allowed to participate. When these new state constitutions were adopted and a majority of southern states had ratified the Fourteenth Amendment, and when that amendment had become part of the Constitution, then the states that had complied with the process would be allowed to seat their delegations in Congress.

The southern state governments established under the Reconstruction Acts of 1867 opened influential roles to black citizens. Black political leaders emphasized the importance of black suffrage and the need for public improvement of all kinds, especially of schools and roads. Whites, however, retained control of the Reconstruction state governments.

Although impeached in 1867, President Johnson survived conviction. In the presidential election of 1868, the powerful Republicans nominated and elected war hero Ulysses S. Grant.
Meanwhile, the physical repair and reconstruction of the South was well under way. But despite
the improvements made by the Reconstruction governments in the states, many white southerners despised them as expensive and northern-dominated. In the long term, the Republicans
were unable to match the organization, experience, and ruthlessness of the conservative defend-
ers of the Old South who sought to "redeem" their region—hence their epithet, the redeemers.
The ruthlessness sometimes took the extreme form of terrorist activity by white-supremacist
organizations such as the Ku Klux Klan. Slowly the Democrats succeeded in "redeeming" the
southern states, and by 1876 only Louisiana, Florida, and South Carolina remained under
Republican administration, kept in power by federal troops.

Nationally, more and more Republicans had come to believe that the defense of black equality
was only an excuse for continued domination by corrupt elements in the party. Support for the
maintenance of Reconstruction dissipated. When southerners in the House of Representatives
supported Republican presidential nominee Rutherford B. Hayes in a controversy over electoral
votes in 1876, Reconstruction had effectively ended. The last federal troops were withdrawn
when Hayes took office the following year.

A. Map Exercises

1. The map reveals several states with governments "set up" during the Lincoln administra-
    tion. Mark them on the map with the letter "L" and list their names. Explain why the
    dates given for their readmission to the Union follow Lincoln's death.

2. The map indicates that all of the remaining states of the former Confederacy had govern-
    ments "set up" during the Johnson presidency. Only some, however, were readmitted
    during the period of Johnson's term in office. Mark them with the designation "J1," and
    list their names. Here again, account for the discrepancy between when the governments
    were "set up" and when the states were readmitted.

3. On the map, mark with the designation "J2" those states from which military control was
    withdrawn during the Johnson administration. List their names.

4. Most of the remaining states saw military control withdrawn during the Grant presidency.
    Mark those states with the letter "G," and list their names.

5. The markings now on the map indicate that Reconstruction began and ended in a strikingly
    fragmentary fashion. The final phase was the withdrawal of federal troops under President
    Hayes. Mark those states with the letter "H," and list their names.

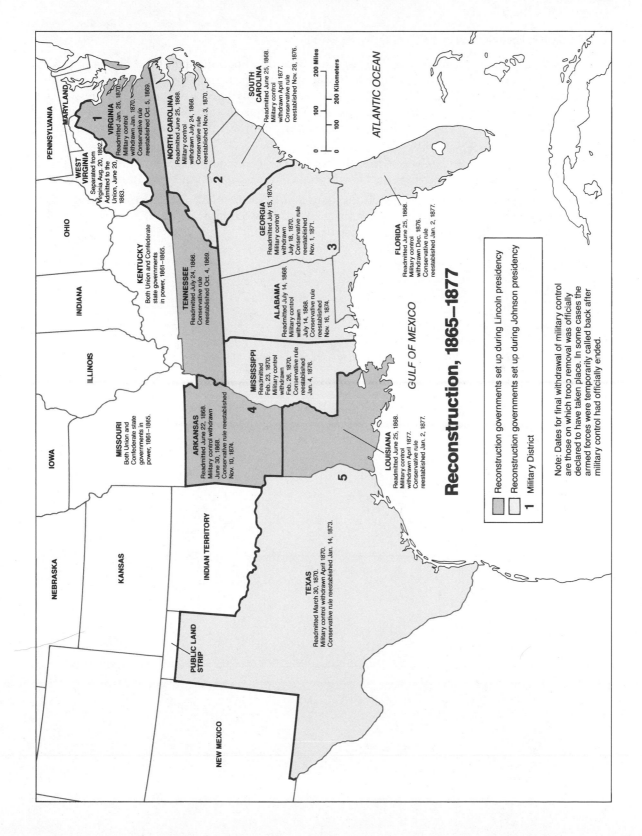

Reconstruction, 1865–1877

ATLANTIC OCEAN

PENNSYLVANIA

MARYLAND

WEST VIRGINIA
Separated from Virginia Aug. 20, 1862. Admitted to the Union, June 20, 1863.

VIRGINIA
Readmitted Jan. 26, 1870. Military control withdrawn Jan. 1870. Conservative rule reestablished Oct. 5, 1869.

1

OHIO

KENTUCKY
Both Union and Confederate state governments in power, 1861–1865.

NORTH CAROLINA
Readmitted June 25, 1868. Military control withdrawn July 24, 1868. Conservative rule reestablished Nov. 3, 1870.

2

SOUTH CAROLINA
Readmitted June 25, 1868. Military control withdrawn April 1877. reestablished Nov. 28, 1876.

INDIANA

ILLINOIS

TENNESSEE
Readmitted July 24, 1866. Conservative rule reestablished Oct. 4, 1869.

GEORGIA
Readmitted July 15, 1870. Military control withdrawn July 18, 1870. Conservative rule reestablished Nov. 1, 1871.

3

FLORIDA
Readmitted June 25, 1868. Military control withdrawn Dec. 1876. Conservative rule reestablished Jan. 2, 1877.

IOWA

MISSOURI
Both Union and Confederate state governments in power, 1861–1865.

ARKANSAS
Readmitted June 22, 1868. Military control withdrawn June 30, 1868. Conservative rule reestablished Nov. 10, 1874.

MISSISSIPPI
Readmitted Feb. 23, 1870. Military control withdrawn Feb. 26, 1870. Conservative rule reestablished Jan. 4, 1876.

4

ALABAMA
Readmitted July 14, 1868. Military control withdrawn July 14, 1868. Conservative rule reestablished Nov. 16, 1874.

GULF OF MEXICO

NEBRASKA

KANSAS

INDIAN TERRITORY

LOUISIANA
Readmitted June 25, 1868. Military control withdrawn April 1877. Conservative rule reestablished Jan. 2, 1877.

5

TEXAS
Readmitted March 30, 1870. Military control withdrawn April 1870. Conservative rule reestablished Jan. 14, 1873.

PUBLIC LAND STRIP

NEW MEXICO

200 Miles
200 Kilometers
100
100
0
0

Reconstruction governments set up during Lincoln presidency

Reconstruction governments set up during Johnson presidency

1 Military District

Note: Dates for final withdrawal of military control are those on which troop removal was officially declared to have taken place. In some cases the armed forces were temporarily called back after military control had officially ended.

B. Further Exercises

1. The dates of the Reconstruction Acts, of the military occupation, and of the return to power of the "redeemers" have not changed. Yet at one time, historians described Reconstruction as harsh and repressive. More recently some historians have stressed its mildness. And most recently, certain studies have interpreted Reconstruction as a lost opportunity, an incomplete effort. Why is it that historical interpretation can take such divergent paths? Speculate on this question in a one-page paper.

2. What were the dates on which the eleven former Confederate states ratified the three Reconstruction amendments to the Constitution? Mark them on the map in each state.

3. As an exercise in memory, mark on the map and label the eleven state capitals of the former Confederacy. For something extra, mark Stone Mountain, Georgia, and research why the locale was significant during Reconstruction.

Glossary

A

acclimatization. The process of becoming adapted to a different climatic environment and, by extension of meaning, adaptation to a whole range of differing economic, cultural, and social conditions.

air mass. A large body of air identified by conditions of temperature and humidity. On the basis of temperature, air masses may be characterized as polar or tropical. On the basis of humidity, they may be characterized as continental (dry) or maritime (moist).

altitude. The vertical distance above mean sea level. Altitude is significant insofar as it affects climate, physical environment, and human activities.

antarctic. Pertaining to the south polar region. The antarctic circle is the parallel of latitude at 66° 32′ S. along which, because of the inclination of the earth's axis, the sun does not set on or about December 21, nor does it rise on or about June 21, the summer and winter solstices.

archipelago. A group of islands in close proximity and usually related geologically.

arctic. Pertaining to the north polar region. The arctic circle is the parallel of latitude at 66° 32′ N. along which, because of the inclination of the earth's axis, the sun does not set on or about June 21, nor does it rise on or about December 21, the summer and winter solstices.

aridity. Dryness; the condition found in a very dry climate, as in desert or semidesert regions.

axis (of the earth). An imaginary line between the north and south poles about which the earth rotates in twenty-four hours. The earth's axis is not vertical but is tilted at an angle of about 66½° to the plane of the ecliptic, the path that the sun appears to follow around the earth in the course of a year.

B

barometer. An instrument that measures atmospheric pressure. The *mercurial barometer* balances the weight of a column of mercury against the weight of a column of atmosphere at a given place and time. At sea level the average weight of a one-inch square column of the earth's atmosphere will support a column of mercury 29.92 inches high; thus, standard atmospheric pressure is 29.92.

bay. A wide curved indentation in a shoreline facing a lake or sea. The word is used as generally descriptive of this feature. Comparatively, a bay is larger than a cove and smaller than a gulf.

borderlands. The area on either side of the boundary between two nations. The term is also used to indicate an area at the edge of settlement.

boundary. A line marking the political limits of control of a given nation. Boundaries may be determined or influenced by the land's physical features, by the differing cultural characteristics of adjacent populations, by the convenience of straight lines formed by parallels and meridians, by war and conquest, and by various combinations of these and other factors.

butte. An isolated hill or rise, especially one with steep sides and a flat top. The word is a western American term.

C

canyon. A steep-sided river gorge. In arid and semiarid regions, such as in parts of the American West, there is little weathering, and so canyons maintain the steepness of their walls.

cape. A prominent portion of land extending into the sea, such as Cape Cod, Massachusetts.

cartography. The science of making maps.

celestial navigation. Determining position, course, and distance by means of observations of the apparent positions of the heavenly bodies.

Celsius temperature scale. A 100-point (centigrade) scale of temperature, named after an eighteenth-century Swedish astronomer, in which, under standard atmospheric pressure, ice thaws at 0° and water boils at 100°. To convert to the Fahrenheit temperature scale, multiply Celsius degrees by 9/5 and add 32.

climate. The total character of weather conditions of a region over an extended period of time. Climate is influenced by latitude and altitude, relative position to land and bodies of water, ocean currents, prevailing winds and atmospheric pressure systems, relief features, and other geographic conditions.

coastal plain. A generally level plain bordering the sea and sloping gently toward it. Coastal plains may vary significantly in width. Some are no more than a narrow strip; others may be much wider, like the broad Atlantic coastal plain that extends south of the Chesapeake Bay region.

compass rose. A directional design used on a map to indicate the points of the compass. The four cardinal directions are shown, together with intermediate directional points—e.g., northeast and east northeast—to a total of thirty-two.

continental shelf. A shallow underwater belt of land that forms a border along the edge of almost every continent. The shelf slopes to a depth of perhaps 600 feet, beyond which there is generally a sharp drop to the ocean floor.

D

dead reckoning. Navigation by means of calculation involving speed, direction, elapsed time, and the effects of wind and ocean currents.

delta. A tract of alluvial sediment created at or near the mouth of a river where the rate of removal by the flowing water is diminished. Deltas have many shapes, and because of their flatness and fertility, they frequently have high value as agricultural land.

desert. An extremely arid region where rainfall is scanty and evaporation exceeds precipitation. On the average, deserts receive less than ten inches of moisture a year.

divide. A high ground between river basins. A drop of rain falling on the precise ridge of the divide theoretically would part to flow in either direction. In North America the *continental divide* separates Pacific and Atlantic drainage.

doldrums. *See* **terrestrial winds.**

drought. Dryness resulting from an extended period without precipitation.

dune. A small hill created by drifted sand, generally windblown.

dust bowl. A semiarid area in which dry, fine surface soil is removed and blown about by the wind. Excessive cultivation or overgrazing may remove the natural ground cover that anchors the soil. Written as a proper name, *Dust Bowl* usually refers to that part of the United States around Oklahoma that has suffered severely from this condition.

dust storm. A wind storm in a semiarid area characterized by dense clouds of dust raised from the surface. Dust storms, marked by low visibility, may be dense enough to produce semidarkness.

E

earthquake. A rapid movement within the earth's crust that sends out shock waves in all directions from the focus, or epicenter. Several regions of the world, especially around the Pacific basin, are particularly vulnerable to earthquakes.

ecliptic. The path followed by the earth around the sun through the year. Visually, it is the apparent path of the sun making a complete revolution around the earth in a year.

ecology. The relationships between living organisms and their environments. The science of ecology is concerned with habits, modes of life, change and development, and mutual interaction.

economic geography. The field of geography that deals with economic resources, patterns of production and distribution, and related matters affected by geographic and spatial features of the earth.

elevation. Height or altitude above a certain level, such as mean sea level.

entrepôt. A center to which goods being traded are brought for storage and subsequent reexportation. The use of New Orleans as an entrepôt was for many years a source of contention between the United States and the nations that once controlled the city, Spain and France.

equator. An imaginary line on the earth's surface, on a plane perpendicular to the earth's axis, midway between the poles. At 0° latitude, the equator divides the earth into two halves, or hemispheres.

erosion. The wearing away of the land surface through movement of the surface materials by agents such as water, wind, waves, and ice.

estuary. The area at the wide mouth of a river meeting the sea where the tide encounters the river's current.

F

Fahrenheit temperature scale. A temperature scale introduced in the eighteenth century. It marks the melting point of ice at 32° and the boiling point of water at 212°. To convert to degrees Celsius, multiply by 5/9 and subtract 32.

fall line. A theoretical line connecting the points at which a series of rivers descend by falls or rapids from a higher to a lower elevation on their way to the sea. The fall line marks the head of navigation for ocean and river vessels. In the eastern United States it separates the Atlantic coastal plain from the piedmont region and early became a location for the transshipment of goods and the establishment of factories powered by water.

fault. A fracture or rupture in the rock strata composing the earth's surface. The San Andreas Fault in California is a very extensive fault line.

floodplain. An area adjacent to a stream or river subject to periodic flooding. Because of fertile silt accumulation, such areas may be attractive for farming. Because of access to river navigation, they may be attractive for urban growth.

foothills. An area of hills lying between a mountain range and a plain.

frontier. (1) The zone between two political entities in the midst of which is the boundary line. Note, however, that *frontier* is sometimes used as synonymous with *boundary*. (2) An area at the edge of settlement facing a less settled or developed area. The U.S. Census Bureau defined a zone with 2 to 6 inhabitants per square mile as the frontier as the nation moved west.

G

gap. A natural cutting through a ridge or series of hills. A gap may become an important pass or route, as did the Cumberland Gap in northeast Tennessee in the eighteenth century, used by Daniel Boone and others.

geography. The study of the earth's surface dealing with areal and spatial relations in regard to physical, biotic, and cultural matters.

Great Basin. The broad interior region of western United States between the Sierra Nevada on the west and the Wasatch Range of the Rocky Mountains on the east. The region is characterized by rugged north-south mountain ranges and a semiarid climate.

Great Central Plain. The region in the interior of the United States, including much of the Mississippi River drainage basin, extending from the Great Plains in the west to the Appalachian Mountains in the east.

great circle. A circle on the earth's surface, the plane of which passes through the earth's center. The shortest distance between any two points on the surface is the arc of a great circle. A great-circle route is a path following the arc of a great circle, such as, for example, the air route from London to Los Angeles that passes over Greenland.

Great Plains. The continental area of central North America that extends eastward from the Rocky Mountains to the region west of the 100° meridian. It is characterized by limited rainfall, short grass, and extensive level areas, although there are some highlands.

greenhouse effect. A popular term that describes the process of heat buildup in the earth's atmosphere. Short-wave radiation passes easily through the atmosphere to the earth's surface. The outgoing long-wave reradiation cannot penetrate the atmosphere as easily. Heat is in this way retained in the atmosphere, much as it is in a greenhouse.

gulch. A narrow, deep ravine with steep sides.

Gulf Stream. An ocean current that originates in the eastern Gulf of Mexico and flows through the Florida Straits and along the eastern coast of the United States, following the edge of the continental shelf to about 40° N., where it turns to flow east across the Atlantic.

H

hemisphere. Half a sphere. The globe is divided into the Northern and Southern hemispheres by the equator. The meridians at 0° and 180° also divide the globe, but the term *Western Hemisphere* is popularly used to mean the Americas.

hill. An elevation of the earth's surface, lower than a mountain. The distinction between a hill and a mountain is imprecise, but the elevation of a hill is generally under 2,000 feet.

hinterland. The backcountry of a coastal settlement. By extension of meaning, a hinterland is any area tributary to a specific location and connected to it by commerce or other interactions.

historical geography. The field of geography that studies physical, biotic (relating to life), and cultural change over time as affected by areal and spatial characteristics of the earth's surface.

horse latitudes. *See* **terrestrial winds.**

human geography. The field of geography especially concerned with human practices and cultural patterns in the context of the geographical environment.

humidity. Generally, the amount of water vapor in the air. *Relative humidity* refers to the ratio, expressed as a percentage, between the amount of water vapor in a given amount of air and the total amount of water vapor the air can hold at that temperature before saturation.

I

ice cap. The large ice mass at either pole. The term is sometimes used for a covering of ice over any tract of land. Generally, the term is reserved for an area notable for its size or physical characteristics, as the ice cap on a mountain.

inset. A small map set within the scope of a larger one. The two maps may or may not be drawn to the same scale.

intermontane. Literally, "between the mountains," a term referring to geographical phenomena that occur between mountain ranges. In the United States the area between the Rocky Mountains and the Sierra Nevada is called the *intermontane West.*

International Date Line. Because the earth rotates from west to east, sun time is always one hour later at 15° east of any given point. Human time must be adjusted accordingly, by means of time zones. The International Date Line at the 180° meridian is the line at which travel from west to east requires setting time back one full day. Similarly, travel from east to west requires setting time ahead one full day.

iso-. Derived from the Greek word for "equal," *iso-* is a prefix used with names of various lines on maps linking points with similar values. Examples include:

    isobar. A line linking points having similar average atmospheric pressure.

    isohyet. A line linking points having similar average precipitation.

    isotherm. A line linking points having similar average temperature.

K

key. *See* **legend.**

L

landform. The shape, form, and nature of a feature of the earth's surface.

latitude. A measure of distance north or south of the equator. There are 90 degrees between the equator and either pole, and one degree of latitude equals approximately 69 miles, or 110 kilometers. Latitude lines, also known as parallels of latitude, proceed poleward from the equator in parallel circles of diminishing circumference described on the surface of the globe.

league. A measure of distance of approximately three miles. Land leagues and marine or sea leagues differ.

legend. An explanation of the symbols, shadings, and colors used on a map. Also called a *key*.

littoral. Referring to a coastal region and generally including both the land along the coast and the water near the coast.

longitude. A measure of distance east or west of the prime meridian, the meridian that passes from pole to pole through Greenwich, England. From the prime meridian, 0°, the other meridians, also known as lines of longitude, are numbered in each direction up to 180°. At the equator the length of a degree of longitude is about 69 miles, or 110 kilometers. As the lines of longitude converge to their meeting points at the poles, the length of a degree of longitude diminishes. At 45°—halfway between the equator and a pole—a degree of longitude is approximately 49 miles, or 79 kilometers, in length.

M

map. A representation of the earth's surface or some portion of it drawn to scale on a plane surface.

map projection. A method of representing on a plane surface, geometrically or by calculation, the geographic features of the spherical earth. Classified by method of construction, the *cylindrical projection* places the map as a cylinder tangent to the globe at the equator, the *conical projection* is to a cone tangent to the globe along one of the parallels, and the *azimuthal projection* is to a plane surface tangent to the globe at a selected point. Classified by attributes, the *equivalent projection* represents areas of any size in correct proportion to one another, the *conformal projection* permits areas to retain the same shape as on the globe, and the *equidistant projection* has all distances from a point or points correct as compared to the globe.

map scale. The ratio between the representation of distance on a map and the actual distance on the surface of the earth.

maritime. Pertaining to the sea. A *maritime climate*, one strongly influenced by an oceanic environment, is found on islands and on the windward shores of continents. The daily and seasonal temperature range is small, and relative humidity is high.

Mediterranean climate. A warm temperate climate found on the western margins of continents in latitudes 30° to 40°. Summers are hot and dry, winters warm and moist. In California such a climate extends inland as far as the coastal mountain ranges.

megalopolis. A densely populated region of settlement formed by the growth of cities and suburban areas in close proximity. The term is often applied specifically to the northeastern seaboard of the United States from southern New Hampshire to northern Virginia. However, it has come to be used generally for areas in which metropolitan centers grow together into larger regions of urban settlement.

meridian. A line of longitude, a great circle that passes through both poles. Meridians are numbered to the east and west from the prime meridian, 0°, which passes through Greenwich, England.

mesa. Tableland. *Mesa* is the Spanish word for "table."

metropolitan area. The region surrounding a city and having a mutual relationship with the life of the city. The Standard Metropolitan Statistical Area (SMSA) established by the U.S. Census Bureau refers to a county or group of contiguous counties (except in New England) of sufficient population, metropolitan character, and degree of integration.

minute. A unit equal to 1/60 of a degree of latitude or longitude. It can be written with the symbol ′, as, for example, in 36° 30′ N.

mountain. A markedly elevated landform, generally with steep slopes and prominent ridges. Mountains are usually so designated when the elevation reaches at least 2,000 feet, or about 600 meters.

mouth (of a stream). The junction of a stream with the body of water into which it flows.

N

natural resources. The wealth provided by nature. Mineral deposits, fertile soil, vegetation, and much else can be included. The list is constantly in flux as human judgment of what constitutes "wealth" changes.

P

panhandle. In the United States, a narrow projection of a state's land out from the state's main land area. Alaska, Oklahoma, and Texas have the most notable panhandles.

parallel of latitude. A line on a map joining all points at an equal distance north or south of the equator and parallel to it.

peninsula. Land nearly surrounded by water and connected to a larger body of land, such as, for example, the Florida peninsula.

physical geography. The field of geography especially concerned with the spatial attributes of climate, landforms, soils, natural vegetation, wildlife, oceans, atmosphere, and their interaction.

physiography. Description and interpretation of topographic features such as hills, mountains, plains, and other relief features of the earth's surface.

piedmont. An area near the base of a mountain range. The eastern edge of the piedmont upland region in eastern United States is the fall line, which is the western limit of the Atlantic coastal plain.

plain. An extensive tract of comparatively flat or gently rolling land. Generally, local relief varies less than 500 feet, the plain itself is less than 2,000 feet above sea level, and there is uniformity of climatic conditions over large areas.

plateau. An upland, sometimes called a *tableland*, with a more or less uniform summit level, usually with an abrupt rise or drop from the surface to adjacent lands. Plateaus generally stand several thousand feet above sea level, but as with plains, local relief varies less than 500 feet.

pole. The north pole and the south pole are the extremities of the earth's axis.

political geography. The field of geography that studies nations, their relationships, and the variations in political phenomena from place to place and region to region in relation to the geographical environment.

prairie. A vast level or rolling area of treeless land occurring in the middle latitudes. In its natural state a prairie develops under an annual rainfall total of 10 to 20 inches and is covered with grass. The U.S. prairie belt is an extraordinarily productive agricultural area.

precipitation. Deposits of atmospheric moisture in the form of rain, snow, sleet, hail, dew, and frost.

prevailing westerlies. *See* **terrestrial winds.**

prevailing winds. The dominant winds at a given latitude.

prime meridian. The meridian or line of longitude of 0° that passes through Greenwich, England, and from which meridians are numbered east or west to 180°. All to the east are east longitude; all to the west are west longitude.

public domain. Land owned by the U.S. government.

R

region. An area on the earth's surface that is marked by similarity of characteristics or features that distinguish it from adjacent areas.

relief. The physical landscape; differences in shapes and forms of the earth's surface. *Relative relief* refers to the highest and lowest points of land in any area. *Local relief* refers to such differentiation in a small area.

right of deposit. The privilege of using a location as an entrepôt (*which see*).

S

sand bar. A ridge of sand or gravel built up in coastal waters, especially near the mouth of a river. A sand bar is at least partially submerged, certainly at high tide.

second. A unit equal to 1/60 of a minute, or 1/360 of a degree of latitude or longitude. It can be written with the symbol ″, as, for example, in 28° 24′ 15″.

semiarid or semidesert climate. A transition zone approaching true desert conditions. In the United States such a climate is found in portions of the Great Basin and the Colorado Plateau. Vegetation is characterized by scrubby bushes, coarse grass, and bare patches.

shelterbelt. A barrier of trees established primarily to protect soil from wind and storm and to prevent erosion.

source. The point where a river rises; the *headwater*.

Standard Metropolitan Statistical Area (SMSA). *See* **metropolitan.**

statute mile. A unit of distance of 5,280 feet.

strait. A narrow water passage connecting two large bodies of water.

sub-. A prefix used to mean "partly." Examples include:

    subarctic. Referring to a region immediately south of the Arctic Circle (66° 32′ N.); by extension of meaning, partly arctic, a region of extreme cold.

    subpolar. Bordering on the polar regions; subarctic; subantarctic.

    subtropical. Bordering on the tropics, nearly tropical.

T

tableland. *See* **plateau.**

temperate. One of the three temperature zones described in classical times, the others being *torrid* and *frigid*. *Temperate* means moderate, but the actual temperature extremes within the temperate zone make the description *mid-latitude* preferable.

terrestrial winds. The wind belts over the earth's surface, generally caused by the earth's rotation, by variation in solar radiation received at the earth's surface, and by alternating high- and low-pressure areas. There are several major terrestrial wind belts. The equatorial belt of variable winds and calms is known as the *doldrums*. Belts of *prevailing westerlies* are located between 30° and 60°N. and S. Northeast and southwest *trade winds* blow more or less steadily equatorward in both hemispheres between 0° and 30°, most strongly at approximately 20° N. and S. Between the trades and the westerlies at about 30° are the *horse latitudes*, two regions, north and south of the equator, of calms and variable winds.

topography. The configurations of surface; all surface features of a given area, including landforms and other aspects.

trade winds. *See* **terrestrial winds.**

tributary. A stream or river that flows into another, usually larger, river.

Tropic of Cancer. The parallel of latitude 23½° N. It marks the northernmost position of the sun's vertical rays, which reach it on or about June 21, the *summer solstice.*

Tropic of Capricorn. The parallel of latitude 23½° S. It marks the southernmost position of the sun's vertical rays, which reach it on or about December 21, the *winter solstice.*

tropics. The portion of the earth lying between the Tropic of Cancer and the Tropic of Capricorn. More generally the word refers to any region of the earth characterized by a tropical—i.e., warm and humid—climate year-round.

V

valley. An elongated depression in the earth's surface, usually associated with a drainage basin.

vegetation. The plant cover of a region; the flora.

volcano. A hill or mountain built up by the ejection of molten material and rock fragments from an opening in the earth's crust. Active volcanoes may expel such materials with great force.

W

weather. The state of the atmosphere at any given time and place, with reference to conditions of temperature, pressure, wind, humidity, cloudiness, sunshine, fog, and precipitation.